A Practical Guide for Christian Mothers:

HOW TO GET ORGANIZED
AND STAY ORGANIZED

A Practical Guide for Christian Mothers:

HOW TO GET ORGANIZED AND STAY ORGANIZED

Cheryl R Carter

JEHONADAH COMMUNICATIONS
Practical publications that make an eternal difference

A division of Foundations for Family Success Ministries
P.O. Box 712
Long Island, New York 11553-0712

Cheryl R. Carter's Jehonadah Communications books are distributed through Foundations for Family Success Ministries. Visit the website at www.FamilySuccess.org or www.Momtime.net.

A Practical guide for Christian mothers:
How to Get Organized and Stay Organized

© Copyright 2006 Cheryl R. Carter
Jehonadah Communications for Foundations for Family Success Ministries
ISBN 0-9669899-2-9

Unless otherwise noted, scripture quotations in this book are taken from the Holy Bible, New International Version® Copyright ©1973, 1978, 1984 by the International Bible Society, used by permission of Zondervan Publishing House. The "NIV" and "New International Version" trademarks are registered in the United States Patent and Trademark Office by the International Bible Society.

All rights reserved. No portion of this book may be reproduced in any form without the written permission of the publisher, except in the case of brief quotations embodied in critical articles or reviews.

The information in this publication is intended for informational purposes only. The recommendations are merely suggestions. The author and publisher assume no responsibility for actions taken as a result of advice in this publication.

*Thank you, Lord Jesus, for your eternal gifts
of Derek, Jarrett, Janae, and Jolene*

Table of Contents

Prayer for our home 9

Introduction
Why a book just for moms? 11

Chapter one
Life management for mothers 15

Chapter two
How to really stay organized! 27

Chapter three
Bringing purpose and order to your home 39

Chapter four
De-cluttering the chaos 53

Chapter five
Cleaning, filing and simplifying 67

Chapter six
Managing ourselves and others 81

Chapter seven
Daily planning 99

Chapter eight
Dealing with procrastination 113

Chapter nine
Productivity boosters 123

Chapter ten
Quick solutions to common problems 137

Chapter eleven
A mother's calling 151

Chapter twelve
Frequently asked time-management questions . .157

Chapter thirteen
Frequently asked home-management questions .165

Chapter fourteen
Frequently asked questions about
    organizing children and teenagers 175

About the author

PRAYER

Lord Jesus, guide me in this special calling to make my home a place where your presence dwells, a safe haven where your word is daily reflected in our activities. May my life and home nourish my family physically, emotionally, and spiritually. May your word be a lamp to my feet and a light to my path as I order my life according to your purposes for my life and my family. In Jesus's name, amen.

Introduction

WHY A BOOK JUST FOR MOMS?

Only God lives in timelessness.

 This book is the kind of book I wish someone had written for me seventeen years ago, when I was still struggling to organize the many facets of my life. Back then, I searched for books on time and home management, but I could not find one that really worked for me. Most organizing books only offered cute anecdotes, trite helpful hints, or complex housecleaning techniques. I remember one system in particular that actually had you write all your household chores on index cards; it further required that you work on those household tasks every day. It was a struggle for me to know what to do and when to do it, so it took me a long time to even record each task I needed to perform on the index cards. Imagine my frustration when I lost the cards. I found it hard to fit into others' organizing systems, yet at the same time, I knew I needed help.

 Was something wrong with me, or the systems I was trying to

fit into? After much prayerful contemplation, I realized I was trying to wear someone else's shoes. Unfortunately, I only determined this after having bought various organizing books, expensive time-management programs, and do-it-yourself cassette tapes. I knew I wasn't the only one who needed help, and I decided to create a system that would work for busy mothers like me, who just wanted to get their homes and lives in order, once and for all.

This book is a result of that quest. In this book, you will learn how to get organized and stay organized. I do not make that assertion rashly, but with a profound understanding that once you make a quality decision to change and get the help you need, you can change. Of course, we lean on the Lord, for he guides us in organizing our lives. When God is in the process, you can do anything, including getting organized. It really just takes a simple godly plan for any of us to succeed. Actually, it is no great secret, for each of us has the capacity to get organized and stay organized when we prayerfully apply a bit of discipline, coupled with a bit of personalization in our homes and private lives. We can actually achieve the peace and order we crave.

Discipline, prayer, and personalization are the three key ingredients to getting organized and staying organized. As moms, we understand the enormity of the task of raising a family. In fact, peace and order can seem elusive at times. However, by having a personal organizing plan, we can gain the solace we so dearly need. This planning process is imperative. It must be engaged in if we are to move from Point A to Point B. We have to grow. Growth is change; anytime we grow, we do so because of planning. This book contains the plan to help transform your life into one of peace and order. This is a personalized plan. It is as unique as you are, because you should not compare yourself to anyone.

Therefore, as you read this book you will see that I do not insist that you do things my way; rather, the thoughts and opinions expressed will help motivate you to find your own personal way of doing things. This is not cookie-cutter life management. This is an exciting process, because you will develop skills that will help you bring order, effectiveness, and peace to your life. In this process, I hope you will also gain a greater vibrancy with God himself, and discover new joy in your family as you are released from the tyranny of your disorganization.

Chapter 1

LIFE MANAGEMENT FOR MOTHERS

*Things do not get better by hoping;
they get better by planning!*

Fundamentally, life management for mothers is the same as for everybody else. The same time-management and organizational principles apply to mothers, and the same skills are necessary for success. However, mothers differ from others in their approach to managing their lives. Mothers tend to be relationship-oriented, and they struggle to balance time between their personal and professional pursuits. This balancing act is tenuous at best, and inevitably, one area of a mom's life seems to suffer. This tension is not something we often speak about, but it is very real.

In addition to balancing their time, elusive expectations permeate mothers in our society. Mothers are encouraged to succeed in a business, raise well-adjusted children, and have great marriages. Even mothers who reject these expectations find it difficult to set their own pace because of societal and church expectations. For instance, the Christian church hails the Proverbs 31 woman as a standard—a nemesis for most women, because her accomplishments seem so unattainable. While many mothers claim to want to be like the Proverbs 31 woman, many cringe each time a sermon reminds them of just how much they do not measure up.

Success for the Christian mother

It also seems that success for the Christian mother is rather elusive, because the "superwoman syndrome" has resulted in mothers striving to reach others' expectations instead of setting their own goals by seeking the heart of God. As a result, mothers often spend their lives living out other people's goals. Ultimately, these mothers end up feeling unfulfilled. Many mothers say things like, "My days are filled with lots of activity, but no meaning." This is usually the result of not knowing who they really are or what they really want. I think all of us have had the experience of running hither and thither because we are not sure what we should be doing. Worse, some mothers become so frustrated and confused that they end up taking on more tasks, in just trying to find meaning in their hurried lives. I engaged in both practices myself.

This may seem rather simplistic, but most mothers do not really take the time to ask themselves what they really want apart from others' expectations. Yet it is essential to discover the perfect plan for our lives, if we are to be organized and thus effective. God created each of us with a plan. He has good plans for us (Jer. 29:11). More importantly, we are part of his greater plan and gifts to humankind in general. As we serve our families, they too discover they are gifts. It is therefore essential that we organize our lives not to become our own gods, but to submit our lives to the lordship of Jesus Christ. Our desire to be more organized actually draws us close to the heart of God, because he is the author of order.

Christian mothers have a tender spot in the heart of God, yet it is we who often feel we never measure up. Perhaps it is because we understand the eternal consequences and missed opportunities of poorly managed time. Perhaps it is because we value our homes and hate to see disorganization gnawing at their foundations. Perhaps it is because we understand that real evangelism begins at home. Perhaps it is because we know our children see Christ through us, and our frazzled responses to their probing questions do not testify of Jesus.

Being a mother is a calling, whether you birthed your children or adopted them. Each child is a gift from God, and the emotional, physical, and spiritual energy you invest in them will eventually yield heavenly returns. It has been said that time is a gift. It is not the time itself but what we put into the time that is the gift. On this side of eternity we are given many things—wealth, prestige, position, wisdom, knowledge, talent, possessions, and accomplishments—but only one thing is destined to remain: our relationships. Our relationships will last into eternity.

Traditional time management has failed us

It is our relationships with those we love that help us to appreciate the concept of eternity. The richness of our lives is measured in the *agape* love we give and receive. As the song says, it was love, not the nails, that kept Jesus on the cross. It is our love for our families that keeps us striving to serve them in excellence. It is this love that must motivate all our time-management and organization efforts.

Traditional time management deals with making lists, maintaining deadlines, and managing others. It is stressed that we should not engage in crisis management—yet so many of our daily mothering tasks often appear to be erratic, firefighter-style time management. The baby cries, and you comfort her. Your son comes home in a talkative mood after winning the great Little League championship, and you take the time to listen while the dust procreates on the piano. Your daughter wants to know if her new haircut makes her look nerdy, and you take the time to encourage her. Is this wasted time? Certainly not! But the truth is that it can seem that way to us, because nurturing and reaffirming our children are not tasks we can necessarily schedule or record in our planners.

We know those tender moments matter, but we miss the experience of triumphantly checking them off our to-do lists like in many other professions. Those tender times are simply not measured in our linear or earthly understanding. When I cry out to Jesus and he hears me, then comforts me, does he mark it off his to-do list? Or does he just relish in our relationship?

Much of Jesus's time was spent in relational pursuits. That is the key to what separates a mother's time from that of all others: she too is, first and foremost, relational. This fact alone is the reason much of traditional time management has failed us. Our time is invested in the lives of our families, so a lot of project-management efficiency rules simply do not apply to us. We have to be careful not to make our families into projects that fit neatly into our personal time slots. It is a struggle, but we must constantly remind ourselves that our efficiency will not always be tangibly calculable. We simply must accept this fact, or we will frustrate ourselves.

More importantly and practically, I think we have to accept the fact that we might not be able to measure our efficiency using checked-off to-do lists. Our productivity is measured by far more divine parameters. We are guided by Jesus's hand. I realize this is a difficult concept to grasp. Still, I really don't think Jesus has a big file on me in heaven, with specific times I can come and speak with him. He says I can call him anytime, and he will answer. Jesus himself stopped to relate personally to all the people he healed. Even though he was on his way to Jarius's house, he stopped to acknowledge the woman with the issue of blood, who was healed. Clearly, she was healed before he publicly addressed her, because the scripture says that he felt virtue leave his body—yet he stopped. He paused to speak to her personally, thereby giving value to her as a person and further affirming the healing.

Does Jesus really understand?

Jesus gave value to the individual by stopping, even in a crowd of people, to speak to one person. Like Jesus, mothers also appreciate relationships. In fact, the gospel is all about our relationship with our Creator. God values relationships. Jesus spent three years in a relationship with twelve men that would ultimately spread the gospel around the world. Think about it. Jesus could have chosen some other method to evangelize the earth, but he chose to invest three years in twelve men.

Jesus did not employ elaborate curriculum plans or diagram flowcharts in the sand. He merely said, "Follow me." And what did these men do? They followed. Yes, they watched him minister, but much of their time was spent observing him eating, sleeping, and praying, and observing the way he related to people. He genuinely cared about people and sought to transfer that concern to his disciples. He could not even send a hungry multitude away. Jesus, like mothers, saw beyond the obvious. He did not look only at the spiritual needs of the crowd, but their physical requirements as well. The disciples learned to really love people from Jesus's example. Might we be able to do the same in our families?

I once heard someone say that Jesus understood mothers. He was followed everywhere he went by twelve guys who gave him no rest. He had to repeat himself over and over again. Even when he was in agony, praying, the disciples were bickering among themselves. Jesus really understands mothers. Remember Jesus the next time you're frustrated because your toddler camps at the bathroom door until you come out, or when you ask yourself, *How many times do I have to repeat myself?* Jesus constantly repeated himself. Jesus, at one point—most likely in frustration or exasperation—remarked, "How long must I be with you?"

Mothering is a truly divine and awesome calling, and we must be careful not to measure our productivity by less-than-divine standards. The needs of our families cannot always be regulated. You may have a diaper-changing schedule, but I can guarantee you that your newborn is not going to stick to it. Much of traditional time management is about getting things done, moving faster. It is product-driven, not relationship-driven. While we can learn from some traditional time-management and organization models, we must always be aware that ministry to our families is best viewed through the lenses of scripture and relationship.

Of course, the application of relational time management brings with it special organizational challenges. As moms, if we are always at our family's beck and call, we will never get anything accomplished. Yet at the same time, if we restrict ourselves to project management and time management, we are sure to be frustrated at every turn. So we will learn to relate to our families and wisely apply some effective time and organizational strategies. First, we must locate where we are on the organizational continuum. This helps us to understand where we need to go.

So where am I?

Before you proceed, I'll like you to understand exactly where you are in terms of organizing your life. My workshop attendees typically fall into one of the following categories, although some people are combinations of more than one type. Let's see if any of these describe you. You will recognize yourself, because you are prone to say the bolded subtitles that follow.

One: How did this happen to me?

You are basically organized, but with each new birth, you find yourself losing ground. You are drowning in a sea of missed opportunities, household chaos, and unrealized goals. You know where you want to go, but are not sure how to get there. You're frustrated, because you're not sure how you got to be where you are, and you simply want to get back to your truly organized self.

You are overwhelmed, and as you read this book, you may find that you have to change your standards. Notice I did not say "lower your standards." The hardest part for you will be to alter your expectations. It will require you to earnestly seek God and ask him how to apply what you are reading to your family and situation. If you try to apply too much all at once, you will become frustrated. Therefore, I urge you to earnestly guard your expectations. Since your natural inclination is to be organized, lean on this strength. Still, you may have to recognize that you have a tendency to be more product-driven than you realize. In particular, pray about shifting your thinking so that you place greater value on relationships than on getting things done or doing more. This will not come easy to you, but eventually you will find that you get more accomplished and are less frustrated.

Pay careful attention to the "managing others" section in this book, because this is perhaps your greatest frustration point. I once met a pastor's wife who confessed to me that in her zeal to be efficient, she had alienated her family from their own home, or place of solace. Her home was immaculate, and her children were on her stringent schedule. As pastoral responsibilities increased, her home was becoming messy. She was upset and reprimanding everyone in the home: child and adult. Finally, in desperation, she insisted on a family meeting. She was certain everyone was equally upset about the perceived mess in the house. Her family told her that they liked the house better messy and were never really happy when it seemed she had it all in order. She confessed that when her house was in perfect order, her children and husband did not like it, because she treated them like they were outsiders trying to invade her neat haven of happiness. The family told her that they merely wanted to enjoy their home. She realized that the mess had occurred because no one really valued the regimenting of the house, as she did. She repented, realizing that everyone should be happy in their home.

Two: It just keeps on piling up!

You were never really organized. In fact, you had a fly-by-the-seat-of-your-pants coping mechanism before you became a mother.

Now, however, your parental responsibilities magnify your disorganization and lack of direction. You are frustrated, because you know you are not reaching your full potential. You are full of creative ideas and have a long mental to-do list, and the truth is that there are so many projects that you want to do. God has placed much in your heart, and you really want to contribute to your home, church, and community, but you just cannot seem to get it together to really do what you want to do. Either you cannot find the time to do those projects, or you feel guilty, like you should be doing something else more worthwhile—like digging yourself out of the mountain of paper on your dining-room table. Your disorganization nags you so much that you cannot pursue other lofty goals.

Since you are so disorganized, you will glean lots from this book. You may already be relationship-oriented, which, unfortunately, may be the cause of your disorganization and poor time management. Therefore, you may need to focus on forming good habits. Sorry, but you also have to stop making excuses for yourself. If it's any consolation, I understand. I was there for many years. I sympathize with you. Like me, you'll have to apply yourself to being consistent in order to get results. Watch for references to how to stay organized, because you have probably read many organizing books, to no avail. Reward yourself even for the little progress that you make, and get a vision for yourself that you really can be personally organized.

Three: There must be something more!

You are organized in most areas. Actually, most of your friends admire your organization and time-management skills. Still, you are not quite satisfied. Is there something you are missing? Perhaps you could be doing more. You cannot put your finger on it, but you have the nagging feeling that you should be accomplishing more, so you're on a quest to find that one organizational technique that will give you that organizational edge you crave.

You will probably glean ideas, but remember to focus on the big picture and not to get upset over details. Remember to invest in your relationships with others and set goals, because organization is never the goal or the objective; it is merely the vehicle that gets you to your destination. Effective time-management and organizing skills should help you achieve your more important, lofty goals. Be careful not to be so perfectionist that you miss out on the things you can achieve. You may be unconsciously engaging in a bit of procrastination due to your perfectionist tendencies. Implement some ideas from this book, but above all, set out to achieve what God has placed in your heart.

Four: But it's not my fault!

You are only reading this book because your husband won't read it, or your children can't read it. You are convinced that it's the kids' fault, or that of your husband or your keen-eyed mother-in-law, who insists on giving your home the white-glove test each time she visits. Really, if everyone else would just get in line and follow your example, they would all be better for it. It is said that you cannot fill the cup of a person who does not realize that her cup is empty. I know it is a hard pill to swallow, but you have to accept the fact that it is you who needs the help. Your husband, kids, and mother-in-law are not reading this book, and therefore I cannot speak to them. I can assure you, the family manager, that you cannot change other people. We can motivate them to change and hope for change, but we can only change ourselves. Therefore, you will have to accept the fact that only you can change yourself, and hopefully your change will motivate others to follow. Changing yourself may just mean employing some new management techniques.

Let's begin

Okay, perhaps you understand something of how you got to be where you are now. At least, I hope you do. As a reminder, relational time management means we employ all the best productivity techniques, but we never elevate a system, method, or technique over our relationships with our families or God. This is most important, because if we study the life of the Proverbs 31 woman, we find that she was a woman who did different things over the course of her lifetime.

The fact that her children called her blessed reveals a major fact that I have heard few sermons address. She had relationships with her children and her husband. We always focus on what she did, but we need to begin to focus on who she was: a woman totally devoted to her family. She placed value on relationships.

This is probably the most important thing to remember. We must always value each other, just like Jesus. As we organize our homes, let us keep Jesus in the forefront, because it is he alone who brings order to our homes. We can employ different techniques, but it is only by his grace that anything works in our homes. As a reformed "messy," I still daily lean on the grace of God to keep my life in order. In fact, I need his grace more when I miss the mark. I wish I could tell you that I never miss the mark and that my home is always in order, but I can't. However, by keeping time management relational and by employing systems, I have learned to get up quickly when I fall. I have also learned that staying organized is an issue few books address. In the next chapter, we will look at the things we must do to stay organized, before we get into the mechanics of time management and organization. Here is the fun relational checklist we use in our family at times:

Fun Family Checklist

- Did I hug everyone today?
- Did I say an encouraging word to everyone today?
- Did I help someone without being asked to do so?
- Did I talk to God today?

- Did I practice self-control today?
- Did I play without bickering today?
- Did I help Mom and Dad today?
- Did I do my chores today?
- Did I do my homework neatly today?

Chapter 2

HOW TO REALLY STAY ORGANIZED!

A habit is something I do without thinking. Good habits are the result of good thinking.

Many mothers tell me how frustrated they are because they get organized and then, after a while, they are right back to their disorganization. It is not enough to get organized, if we cannot stay organized. In fact, it just breeds more frustration and discouragement when we just cannot stay organized. Maintaining organization in our lives takes skill, tact, and determination. We need genuine change to occur.

Real change

Change primarily takes place in the following steps. First, we become aware that we need to change. At this point, we may recognize the pain of our disorganization; it may be lost opportunities, unfulfilled relationships, or simply a lack of peace. Next, we acknowledge that we need to change. First we are honest with ourselves, and then we confess our fault to others. This is essential, because no one can change when she is in self-denial. Twelve-step programs hinge on this fact. All of us have heard the classic story of an alcoholic who thinks he or she can stop drinking at any time. The truth is that the alcohol controls the individual, and until the person faces this reality, he or she can never be truly free. No one can change until she admits a problem exists. It must be affirmed that you cannot heal a thing by saying it does not exist.

After we have acknowledged that we need to change, we must engage a plan to change. Good intentions do not help us. Each of needs applied persistent action, or steps to take to reach our goal, so we prepare by having a realistic plan of action that is simple to implement. Complicated plans only frustrate us, and all plans should be birthed in prayer. The plan must also have follow-through and guide us into developing new habits. Likewise, accountability and reward are parts of any good plan. It may seem a bit clinical to say so, but the elements of preparation and planning are important if that decision is to be actualized. We start at the beginning.

Addressing the roots of why we are disorganized will help us more than simply looking for another organizing or time-management technique. Many mothers embarrassingly confess that they are closet organizing-book junkies. They keep reading, thinking something will stick one day. They try new methods, but soon fall off the proverbial organizing horse. Then, in frustration, they buy another book, convinced that a new technique will help them get organized. This does not work. If we want to break out of the cycle from messy to organized, then we have to get at the root of why we fluctuate. We need perspective on why we cannot stay organized.

Seeing the same thing all the time

Moses faced a similar dilemma. In Psalms 90:12, he prayed, "Teach us to number our days, so that we may gain a heart of wisdom..." The Hebrew prophet Moses penned these words at a time when the children of Israel were aimlessly circling the mountain in the wilderness. It probably seemed to them like their days had little significance. They saw the same thing every day. In the monotonousness of their days, I am sure they began to question whether their lives had meaning. They probably struggled with some of the same thoughts we face in the seemingly repetitive activity of our days.

This scripture is noteworthy because it reflects a core belief in the heart of Moses, their leader. He longed for his life and the lives of his followers to have meaning. He knew the pain of aimless wandering, for he had already spent forty years in the desert, running from the will of God. After Moses accepted the call to be the deliverer of the Israelite people, his life took on new meaning. Moses wanted to make sure neither he nor any of the other Israelites ever missed out on the will of God again.

Moses wanted to know he was doing the right thing at the right time. Wisdom is the result of time and activity producing a desired result. Essentially, that is what we all want for our lives. As we look at the scripture, it is noted the original word "number" in Hebrew is derived from the word *manah*, which means "to allot, enumerate, or organize." Moses wanted to know how to organize his days to live a fulfilled life in the allotted time given him. He wanted to live out the measure of his days in activities and gratifying relationships, which God had ordained. Thus he would be fulfilled each day.

Truly, our lives are composed of our days. Our life is the sum total of our days. It behooves us to live each day with purpose. Like Moses, we should say, "Teach me to organize my life, so that I can know to do the right thing at the right time."

Moses understood that wisdom begins in the way we successfully handle our daily lives. Wisdom's results are profound, yet wisdom is revealed in the seeds of our daily decisions. Those who lead successful lives do so as the result of managing their days proficiently. Our daily lives should bring us closer to the realization of personal success. It all begins with a plan.

The specific plan of God for your life is within you. It can be drawn out of you, like a fine sculptor can turn a lump of clay into a fabulous work of art. Only you hold your own chisel. You must find your own hidden treasure. You must find meaning and purpose for your life. It all begins with an appreciation of time. Moses understood that time is a self-contained entity. You cannot control the way it flows in or out. We cannot manage it like money, but we can manage ourselves—getting more out of the time that we do have available to us. We all have the capacity to live more purposefully. We merely have to look at those areas in our lives that keep us from getting organized and staying organized. Here are a few reasons why most of us don't remain organized.

We have not developed systems to keep us organized.

People need systems to help them stay organized. Systems are a way to approach something. It can be something in our environment, or the way we spend our time. Systems help us, because we have something to fall back on. In essence, they are our security blankets, because we know what to do before events happen. Generally, when we are reading the mail, we don't think about it, at least not at that moment. Instead, we just drop the mail someplace and later figure out what to do with the ensuing mess. The key to a successful system is that it must be individually tailored and easy to implement. It must take into account our human frailties and natural tendencies. We gravitate to the easy. This book is simplified so that you can easily adapt the systems to your life, so you will continually use them.

We are not honest with ourselves.

In order to stay organized, we must honestly look at our bad habits, and the systems we adapt must take into account those tendencies. For instance, if I have the tendency to throw my clothes on the bedroom floor, I might ask myself what the circumstances are that cause me to carelessly toss my garments. Am I tired, stressed, or just plain unmotivated? Sometimes it is a hard call. Whatever the case, I have to address the reason, then adapt a system that will help me with that behavior and motivate me not to engage in destructive behavior that keeps me from my goals. No one can do this for me. I must be honest with myself.

Honesty is at the core of any significant change. If we deny our character flaws, we are doomed to forever repeat them. Someone once asked me if I had ever met just plain old lazy people who were destined to be disorganized. In my fourteen years as a professional organizer, I have rarely met lazy people. I have met overwhelmed, discouraged, stressed, and unmotivated people, but few lazy people.

We moms tend to be really hard on ourselves. We have unrealistic expectations of ourselves. Most of us have fallen into the "supermom" syndrome, and we have very high standards and find it difficult to release ourselves from them. We have to recognize that our standards are just not realistic, and therefore unobtainable. I have never met a person, including myself, who was perfectly organized in every aspect of her life.

We are unable to adapt to change.

Change happens to all of us; it is the only constant in our lives. All of us are changing daily, and as we change, we adapt our systems and environments to reflect those changes. A mother with an active toddler who can get into everything must childproof her home in ways she never could have imagined when that child was a squirmy infant who liked to be held.

Change is inevitable. We have to anticipate changes and adapt to them to keep ourselves organized. If you are the mom of a wiry toddler and insist on operating as you did when your child was an infant, you will only frustrate yourself. All organization strategies, like us, must evolve and change as the dynamics of our personal and family lives change. It is necessary to remember that changes in your lifestyle, no matter how slight, should trigger changes in the way you organize your environment or manage your home.

We are under too much stress to change.

Stress affects our productivity because it inhibits our ability to reason effectively and takes a toll on our bodies. Not surprisingly, doctors today report that many of our illnesses are self-inflicted through stress, poor diet, and unresolved conflicts. All of us live with some degree of stress in our lives; it is virtually unavoidable. However, we need to be aware when we are under stress and adjust ourselves accordingly.

High stress quotients have been assigned to some things like having a baby, moving, starting a new job, and applying for credit. When we are engulfed in stress, we have to change our systems, or relax (perhaps alter) our standards so that we can still be effective. However, we moms tend to heap more guilt on ourselves and try to go on as we did before we became stressed.

Once we recognize stress, then we are able to realistically determine our limits and organize ourselves around those limits. Once, when we were going through major renovations on our home, I realized that my meal-management system had to be altered, because I did not have time or space for meal preparation. I adapted to a different meal plan, instead of beating myself up about not being able to cook like I used to before renovations had begun. I wish I could say I always approach problems like this. Unfortunately, I do not. I am learning to ask myself, when things totally fall apart, if I am just too stressed.

We do not have an accountability partner.

It's funny: we have accountability groups for almost every problem today except organization. That's a shame, because most of us just need a bit of motivation to clean up our acts, so to speak. After all, the last time you had company, you probably cleaned your house from top to bottom. The embarrassment or pride (whichever you choose) motivated you to get the job done, no matter how tired you may have been. Women in particular erroneously find their identities in their homes, and thus find it difficult to let others know about their struggles to keep a clean house. Even those brave souls who do admit they need help will still often gravitate to others like themselves.

A pact with a friend can be a real catalyst for getting organized and staying organized. In my workshops, I encourage moms to become one another's accountability partners. I have found that friends who attend my workshops together are most likely to keep up their newfound organizational skills. Friends help to encourage us, and occasionally spur us with a bit of good-humored competition. Accountability can be pint-sized too; even my kids have kept me accountable.

We engage in self-defeating talk.

What we say to ourselves really matters. We speak to ourselves at the rate of about one thousand and five hundred words per minute. Of course, we are able to articulate at far less speed. It is the things we say to ourselves unconsciously that we have to be aware of. In Proverbs, it states that as a man thinks, so is he (Prov. 23:7, KJV). In other words, you believe whatever you habitually say to yourself. This is not surprising.

Social scientists have long told us that if we say something often enough, we began to believe it. Thus it is what we say to ourselves—particularly those things we say habitually or unawares—that we need to be concerned about. Sometimes we say things like, "I'll never be organized. I was born this way." Or we say, "Other people can change, but not me." This kind of unfruitful conversation seals your doom, because it likewise produces a vision of failure in your organizing efforts. You see yourself as a failure, and then you fail, because your own words have produced an image of impossibility for you. Therefore, you need positive affirmations of your success, despite your past failures.

We do not recognize the bumps in the road.

I suppose there is a more accurate psychological term for this, but I cannot think of a more adequate way to describe this phenomenon. It occurs when we ignore the obvious and do not adapt to compensate for the inevitable. For instance, perhaps you notice that when you are tired, you tend to toss your dirty clothes on the floor. You can leave them there on the floor, or you can compensate for your tiredness by having a place to put your clothes when you are tired. It is like seeing the bumps in the road. You slow down, so as not to damage your car. We all need to recognize the weakness in our characters or schedules, and adapt accordingly.

We are just not practical enough.

As a recovering "messy," I think this is where I still have my challenges: trying to fit into someone else's plan. Years ago, I got hold of an organization book in which the author suggested purchasing index cards and writing all your household tasks on them. First of all, I was not even aware of what household chores I was supposed to be doing in my home. It took me considerable time to figure out what I was supposed to be doing, but the clincher was that I lost the cards. It was someone else's system, and it did not work for me. This is the biggest reason why most people buy organizing books. They are always trying to use someone else's systems, instead of using them as springboards to develop personalized systems. While I will offer you many ideas, remember to use my ideas as a launching pad for your own personal system.

We are caught in the blame game.

When we think our problems are other people's fault, we look for them to change. We make ourselves victims, and immobilize ourselves with this thinking. Many moms come to my workshop and tell me their problems are entirely their husband's fault, or that of the kids, or the old dog...well, you get the picture. You cannot change other people. You can motivate them to change. You can invite them to change. You can even beg them to change, but the only person you can change is yourself. So if you get caught in thinking "it's the kids fault" or "it's my husbands' fault," it keeps you from looking at yourself so you can change.

We have an impossible picture in view.

While a perfectly ordered house may be desirable, it might not be possible if you have three preschoolers, are home-schooling, and are running a home business. Therefore, you have to relax your standards and adapt to those things you can order. Sometimes we are so idealistic that we do not see reality. Once I got a frantic call from a client whose office desk, as she described it, was organized chaos. I prepared for the worst. When I got there, I discovered the desk was actually very orderly. It was just that she was working for a busy counseling agency that had received a large influx of clients. In fact, she was ministering to the needs of the callers by giving them encouragement and time; she was even keeping accurate correspondence logs. As I saw it, there was little she could do beyond what she had already done, given the scope of her job. Nonetheless, she had an idealistic picture in mind that was frustrating her.

We forget organizing should be relational.

The main reason I see mothers failing to stay organized is because they do not realize their jobs are more relational. It is easy to handle papers, numbers, and stuff, but our kids don't come in neat little packages to be organized. Children are messy, unpredictable, and illogical. This is not taken into account in most time-management and organizing books or programs. We neglect this obvious fact ourselves at times. One client once told me she was constantly annoyed by some of the work-at-home magazines she saw that showed angelic toddlers sitting on their mothers' laps while they typed. Her children were reckless, she confessed. They banged on her keyboard, rolled on the floor (to get her attention), and wanted her to read them "The Cat in the Hat" at least five times a day.

As we talked, she realized that she had not been spending enough time with them, and she hadn't established boundaries that toddlers could understand. Toddlers understand literal physical barriers and concrete, measurable time frames. I suggested using a timer that they could look at, and scheduling reading times. She also set up a play office for them. It was simple; once she had accepted that toddlers vie for attention, she was able to spend time with them, and adapt her schedule so that they everyone was happier.

We are not hurting enough.

I purposely saved this one, but it is the harshest concept to accept. Sometimes our disorganization gnaws at us, but it is not bothersome enough for us to really change. We read a book or take a class but make no effort to change because it is not a major issue in our lives. Some people take my classes who really don't want to be there. They were urged to do so by concerned spouses, parents, friends, or children, but they really have no vested interest in getting organized, because it really is not a major issue to them. It is like the story about the farmer and the old hound dog who is sitting on the porch howling in pain. A neighbor passes by and asks why the dog is howling. Obviously, he is in pain. The farmer replies that he is sitting on an old nail. "Why doesn't he get up?" asks the neighbor. "I guess it does not hurt enough yet," remarks the farmer.

Our disorganization has to hurt us enough to make us really want to change, so that we will do anything to resolve the issue. Perhaps your past efforts to get organized have discouraged you. Once, we were supposed to move out of our home, and it was to be demolished. I found it difficult to motivate myself to clean or organize my home, because I knew it was coming down. In addition, repairs were badly needed throughout the house, but since we knew we were moving, we had neglected them too. Needless to say, the environment was very discouraging. Every day the situation got worse. In addition, the contractor delayed the project for over a year, and I was partially packed, based on his ever-deceptive time frames. It was the worst time for our family, and I had to learn to live in chaos. One day, I realized I had been adapting to chaos and hopelessness. I resolved to clean and organize the house, even if it meant the house would not be showcase-perfect. After the house was organized, my mindset changed; I became more positive. Our environment really does affect us.

In the next chapter, we will get down to the nitty-gritty of organizing our homes so that we can be at peace.

Five Keys to Successful Change

One **Become aware you need to change and make a decision to do so.**
You become uncomfortable, irritated or down right angry with change that needs to take place in your life. You realize it is a problem.

Two **Acknowledge and make a decision to change.**
You make a public confession to others and to yourself that change is imperative. We are committed to what we verbally declare to others. You no longer deny the problem or the effects your problem has on you and others. Most important you stop making excuses.

Three **Prepare and plan for change.**
You accept the fact there will be obstacles to your good intentions. You therefore anticipate those obstacles then move ahead to address them so they do not impede your progress. You make a realistic plan

Four **Strengthen your resolve to change with accountability. Follow-through and Accountability**
You recognize you will need follow-up. Follow-up may take days, months or years. Decide on a specific barometer to measure your progress. Get someone to be accountable to for your change. Discipline requires accountability.

Five **Reward yourself for even the little steps.**
You give yourself a tangible or emotional pat on the back each time you make even a small step of progress.

Chapter 3

BRINGING PURPOSE AND ORDER TO OUR HOMES

Purpose must always precede order.

Now that we understand that, for mothers, time is relational first, and now that we are aware of some hindrances to our remaining organizing, let's begin the process of organizing our lives. We will begin in our homes. I used to help mothers with their time-management skills first and then advance to home organization. However, I have found that most mothers need to have uncluttered, clean environments before they can think clearly about anything. Haven't you ever cleaned your house from top to bottom and simply enjoyed just walking in each room, regaling in your accomplishment? You are able to think better and feel better just by being in an orderly home. It just makes you feel good.

We begin by asking ourselves: how would we like our homes to be remembered? This question helps us to identify the positive aspects of our home, and sets the parameters for all our organizing efforts. Often, in the excitement of bringing order to our homes, we mistakably extract the life or vibrancy of the place. For instance, if you like sewing, and have homemade items throughout your house, you should not get rid of all of your beautiful handmade pieces; you merely have to organize them neatly. Yes, you will need to purge some items, but you do not have to lose the personality of your home in the purging process.

You may want to write your own home mission statement. This statement will identify your values and address the more important aspects of how organizing your home will better serve you and your family. I encourage all mothers to write mission statements for their homes, because it helps focus our energies on why we really want to organize our homes. It is important to remember that an organized home should not be the sole goal of any family. An organized home should serve a much loftier goal of hospitality, evangelism, or outreach ministry.

Organizing is just the vehicle that helps us reach our destinations. Therefore, we should always know why we are taking the time to get our lives in order. A home mission statement helps us not to get sidetracked in our organizing efforts, and helps to keep our larger goals foremost in our minds. For instance, I post my mission statement to remind me why I want to stay organized. My family home mission statement is the following:

To create an environment where:
A relationship with God is encouraged and family members
   are nurtured emotionally;
A love for learning is fostered;
Each family member develops physically;
Joy resonates in each room; and
All family members are able to exercise their God-given talents,
   gifts, and abilities to reach their full potentials.

Okay, it may seem a little syrupy, but you get the idea. Focus on what qualities you want developed in your home, or how you want your home remembered. You may keep it short, or use a bible verse to magnify the meaning. I summarize my mission statement this way: "To create an environment where all continue to grow in wisdom, stature, and favor with God and mankind." By rewording it in brief, I can easily remember it. This is not absolutely necessary, but it does help me.

Clarity and conciseness is important. Your mission statement should be clear to you, and you should be able to explain it to others, particularly other family members. Perhaps you can discuss it with your husband, or have a family meeting. Your mission statement should be clear, and it should be written down. Put it in your own words, so that it can inspire you. Foremost, it must be significant to you.

Others are more apt to cooperate with you when they understand what you want to accomplish. A mission statement helps to center your desires so that your goal is more than just keeping the house clean. Ask yourself why you want an orderly home. Check your motives. Be clear and honest with yourself. This will involve taking the time to really think about your values and being open before the Lord.

As you think of your home, how do you want it to be remembered? What do you want your children to say about your home? How would others characterize your home? What is really important to you? What major activities take place in your home? All these questions are important, because the answers reveal your values and the characteristics of your home. This assessment may seem unimportant, but the answers will guide you in permanent change.

Most likely, you are reading this book because you are ready for positive changes in your home. Define for yourself what those changes are right now. Take a moment to see those changes. If your home were to be completely organized, how would those changes make you feel? Allow yourself to feel those emotions. Emotions can be powerful motivators. They can motivate you to move toward the changes you desire. I really want you to be aware of what is genuinely motivating you to make needed changes.

Your motivations are important, because you are the home manager and therefore the catalyst for change in your home. Your home should be managed like a business with you as the chief executive officer (CEO) and head of quality control. In fact, the home can arguably be considered the best-managed business in the world today.

Just as every business is different, every home is different. The purpose for your home is different from that of anyone else's home. Every family has different values and priorities. Also, the personality of your home may dictate a different approach from that of another home with a similar family structure or activities. Every home reflects its occupants' personal values and unique priorities.

Homes also have personal characteristics that are unique to them. These characteristics affect the overall flow of the home. A personal characteristic or individual flavor is a distinct quality which affects every area of the home. Is your husband a doctor with unpredictable hours? Is your daughter training for the Olympics? For instance, in my home, a love for God, family, people, and learning is stressed. These qualities are reflected in our lifestyles, first as Christians, then as counselors, home-educators, and ministry workers. What are the personal characteristics of your home and family? Think about it.

Your home should serve you

I once heard a mom say, "If you want to see me, come over anytime, but if you want to see my house, you will have to make an appointment." She made this statement because she was determined to make her home as hospitable as possible, but she did not want to spend all her time cleaning it. It is funny how many of us will clean our homes just for company, when our families live in squalor. However, our homes should be organized primarily for our families, secondarily for others. We communicate the wrong message to our families when we only put out the good china for guests. Our families are our first and most important ministry.

Your home should serve you. You should never serve it. Everything in your home should bring you closer to your family goals. Your home also reflects your values. In fact, you have to take a decisive look at your values, because sometimes the disorder in your home can be attributed to those values. For instance, you may encourage scientific inquiry, and your home may reflect this by having scientific paraphernalia all over the place. If this is the case, your home might not be as neat as you want it, but you may be proud that your children are growing intellectually through scientific experimentation. Understanding this will help you address the disorder issue in the context of your family's values and the more important aspects of your family life.

Purpose precedes order

As we have already determined, if we want to get organized and stay organized, we have to recognize that all disorganization is the result of confusion. Confusion is better defined as a lack of purpose. Purpose is simply the reason why something exists. It sounds a bit ethereal, but stay with me for a moment, and you'll understand exactly what I mean by that statement. Purpose is the foundation of all order. If you want to get any area of your life in order, you must understand the purpose for that thing, relationship, or idea.

The concept of purpose is better understood as we see it applied to our homes. Perhaps you carelessly toss papers on your dining-room table. Is it a table, or a desk? How are you using it? Are you violating its purpose? It sounds rather crass, doesn't it? In my organizing workshops, I often get a chuckle when I share this principle: if the purpose of a thing is not clearly understood, then abuse is inevitable. I follow this statement with the example that a dining-room table is not a desk. If papers are tossed on it haphazardly, then its purpose gets violated, and you have a mess. You cannot treat a dining-room table like a desk and expect it to remain neat, because tossing the paper on it violates the purpose of the table.

I first heard this principle from Dr. Myles Monroe of Bahamas Faith Ministries as he discussed the relationship between husband and wife. However, as I meditated on the principle, I realized that it applied to equally to household management and organization, because all order is preceded by purpose. If you want to get any area of your life in order, you have to understand its purpose. Think about it. Everything in our lives has a purpose, and when we cooperate with that purpose, we have order.

Once we have order, we can find rest, because all of instinctually crave order. That order is always preceded by purpose. There is beauty in order. An ordered environment helps us think clearer. In fact, a cluttered environment breeds confusion. It had been proven that we naturally think clearer and better in clear, uncluttered surroundings. Even our kids gravitate to the areas we clean, after they overwhelm their own living spaces with clutter. It annoys us, because it seems like they are undoing all our hard work. However, it helps us to understand that even children crave order; we need to help them by showing them how to keep order in their personal spaces too.

Each of our homes possesses its own character. As I stated earlier, we do not want to regiment the life out of our homes. A hospital may be clean and orderly, but it is also sterile and antiseptic and cold. It has no life. No one wants to spend a lot of time in a hospital. Every home has a character, because every family has its own values, or things deemed important to that family. Do not assume that families with similar dynamics will have homes with the same character.

One of my dear friends has kids the same age as my kids, and for the most part, we have similar values. In fact, our husbands share comparable activities, yet our homes are ordered quite differently. She enjoys cooking, and her house is ordered around her activities in the kitchen, whereas I dislike cooking, and spend more time in other areas of my home.

Understanding your home's purpose

Every room and space in a house has a purpose. If that purpose is violated, the result is disorder or a mess. Now that we understand that, let's get to work bringing order to our homes. First, look at the chart at the end of this chapter. You will notice that it has three columns, titled Room/ Space, Purpose, and Activities. Photocopy this chart, because you will be using it frequently. You will revise it frequently, as your kids are going to get older, and you will be working toward different goals. To stay organized, you have to constantly assess where you currently are in relationship to keeping your home in order.

Let's get back to the chart. First, choose a room in your home. Let's pick the kitchen, because it is generally the most active room in any house. You will notice that the kitchen part has been filled in on your chart as an example. This in no way implies that the purpose of your kitchen is the same as the purpose in the example. In fact, it should be different, because purpose is personal and evolves out of the intimate character of our homes.

Many organizing books or programs provide cookie-cutter time management. They assume we all should organize the same way. This is just not true. Each of us is an individual, and if we want to stay organized, we have to adapt any system to our own personalities, temperaments, and family needs. When we attempt to fit into someone else's system, we stay with it for a little while, then throw our hands up in exasperation and gravitate to the familiar. Unfortunately, for most of us, the familiar is a place of disorder. So let's avoid failures by not haphazardly adopting anyone's regimented system.

Now let's look at our example kitchen. Notice our sample family is a family of eight. This mom complained that her kitchen is the messiest room in the house. This family cooks in the kitchen, opens mail, does homework, plays games, meets with friends, watches television, and finally, yes, they eat there too. Is it any wonder that this kitchen is a mess? There are so many activities going on in the kitchen. There should be one, perhaps two purposes tops for most of the rooms in your house. In this case, I helped the mom narrow the activities in her kitchen by determining her purpose.

The purpose for this mom was to have a space where everyone could eat and be together as a family. However, she realized that her family rarely used the kitchen as a meeting place, because it was so cluttered and uncomfortable. When everyone was in her tiny kitchen, they were usually cattily bickering, because everyone was bumping into each other. We narrowed her kitchen's purpose significantly to include only essential activities, such as cooking and homework. Since the family was large, they also agreed that the kitchen table was one place everyone could be quiet and do homework.

After we established the purpose of the kitchen, we went through each room in the home and repurposed it. The key is to limit the number of activities in each room. In the Farrell home, we had to cut back on the rooms the children were allowed to play in, because it resulted in toys being cluttered throughout the whole house. In my home, we have a tendency to leave books all around the house, so I limited the kinds of books my kids could read in certain rooms in our home. My children are only allowed to read library books in our family room, right next to the library-book box, which is strategically placed in that room.

The most effective way to bring purpose to your home is to take the chart and go through each room in your home, identifying the activities that occur in them. I used to advise moms to note the purpose of the room and then the activities. However, over the years, women have told me it was easier for them to note the activities in each room and then determine the rooms' purposes, especially if their homes were really disorganized. They simply did not know where to begin, but they were able to identify what was going on in each room.

Be honest when you initially note the purpose and activity of each room. Write down what is actually occurring, not what you want to happen in each particular room. Honesty is the core of change. Nothing in our lives will change unless we are honest. Once you have a clear and genuine assessment of what activities are occurring in each room of your home, you are ready to organize your home. Look at your chart. Circle the activities that are happening in more than one room. Are there multiple places to watch television? Are there books in every room? Do you constantly find cups and saucers all over the house, because snacking is taking place in many rooms? Determine what activities you will eliminate and which ones you will accommodate in each room.

Remember that your purpose is unique. Each room in your house has a distinct purpose. Purpose is not all-inclusive. Purpose is related to the personal characteristics and personality of your home. For instance, most kitchens are used for meal preparation and eating. Currently, this is not the sole purpose of my kitchen. My kitchen is a classroom and a family meeting place. My kitchen is designed with those purposes in mind. The decor and layout reflect this purpose. We have a wipe-board, part of the family library, and toys in the kitchen. It is one of the places where we home-school. That may stun some of you, but it works for us. In order for this purpose exercise to be beneficial, you must throw protocol out the window. Find out what is right for you, and follow through.

A *place for everything*

When the purpose of a space is violated, disorder occurs. All disorder is caused by a violation of purpose; therefore, we must employ the process of accommodation or elimination. It is a simple process. You simply eliminate those activities or items that are upsetting the order of your home. For example, if the mail is constantly cluttering the kitchen counter, then it needs to be eliminated. The process of opening and receiving mail in the kitchen will have to be evaluated. An alternative system for receiving and reading mail can be adopted, or opening the mail in the kitchen can be eliminated totally.

Remember, this process is so personal that no one can tell you what you should get rid of or hold onto. It is your personal decision. This is a personalized blueprint for your home. You decide what you are willing to accommodate and what you feel you need to eliminate. How do you decide to accommodate or eliminate? It is very simple: use the values in your mission statement as a guide, or simply follow your heart. One time, I realized our family needed a place for solitude, so I made our guest room a quiet room. I put a fish tank and a few special books in the room. It was a real blessing to our family at that time. As our family grew, I had to give up that space to accommodate other family activities.

Remember, your accommodation/elimination plan must work for you. Convenience is the foundation. While most people would put bibs in the dresser drawer in the nursery, it was not the closest point of use for me. I put them in a convenient place. At one point, I put them in my china closet because that was the room I was in when I needed a baby's bib. Think out of the box. Think of your convenience, not social protocol. Convenience, or ease, should always take preference. Likewise, make it easy for children to do tasks. If you want your children to hang up their coats, do they have hooks they can easily reach?

Abandon typical protocol in favor of convenience and ease, as this will help you to maintain your organizing momentum when you are tempted to give up. While I am not recommending that you keep pots and pans in the bathroom, I am suggesting that you really give some thought to why you do the things you do. Reassess all your activities, because this also helps you to stay organized. Ask yourself what makes you the most productive. If you have a work desk, but always end up at the dining-room table doing work, then something is wrong. Perhaps it would be better to relocate your desk or to change the purpose of the table. Be flexible and creative when problem-solving.

Ask yourself why you do certain things. I once had my home office in the basement, but generally carried my clients' papers around the house with me in my portable files. I realized that I did not like working in the basement, because it was dark and it kept me away from people. When I relocated my desk to my bedroom, my productivity soared, although all the work-at-home books I had read advised that you never locate your work space in your personal space. Some people tell me they cannot work around others, but it was quite the opposite for me.

It almost seems too obvious to mention, but I will say it anyway: there must be a place for everything. You've probably heard it before. As you are repurposing the rooms in your house, take a moment to note the messes. What things are accumulating? Books? Mail? Magazines? Toys? What things need specified places in each room? Absolutely *everything* needs a proper place to maintain order.

When my children were young, I often told them to put items back in their "homes" (specific places they were to be stored), to help them understand the importance of order. This concept of putting things back where they belong has helped over the years. To keep everyone organized, always place things at the point of use, where it is easy to retrieve them. Also, be certain that everyone agrees on an item's home.

As a rule, you should try to compartmentalize as much as possible, by which I mean to have a separate space for each item.

For instance, I have all of my first-aid items together, so that if anyone has an accident, I do not have to look for the alcohol in one place and the Band-Aids in another. I compartmentalize my baby items, contact lens and eyewear, etc. This helps to keep things very orderly, and can help you to gain cooperation from the rest of the family, because they do not have to look for small items.

Small items should be stored in larger, easy-to-find items like bins or baskets. Baskets are also very helpful if there are items that are used by more than one family member in different parts of the house. For instance, I have a small basket that contains different nail clippers and files. It is easier to locate a basket than to try to find tiny nail clippers or tweezers. Baskets can also be used for hairbrushes, safety pins, and the like—whatever items the family uses as a whole. I also find that crates are sturdy and handy for storing toys, books, and cleaning supplies.

Remember that you will frequently need to use the chart to reorganize your home. As your children grow and you adopt new activities, you will find that you will need to repurpose some of the rooms in your home.

Sample Family: Farrell Family – Utilizing the Purpose Chart

Room/Space	Purpose	Activities
Kitchen	?????	Watch television, play games, kids play with toys, entertain team after games, open mail, cook meals, make lunches, open mail, eat meals, kids do homework at table, watch television
Kitchen	Meal prep and organized family meeting place	Meal preparation, quiet homework zone, family communication center

For Your Own Use

Room/Space	Purpose	Activities

Quick Tips

- Write down the purpose of each room. You want to identify the purpose or the intent—why that room exists in your home.
- Write down as many activities you can think of that occur in the room.
- Activities are concrete. You should be able to state it specifically. Suppose the purpose of your basement is to have a quiet space for the family. The activities are what you do in that room, like playing games and snacking. Activities should not be vague.
- Be honest with yourself. If a room exists purely for vanity and no one goes into it except to clean, then say so.
- Write the purpose in your own vernacular. You are not trying to impress anyone.
- If you notice that your purpose and activities are incongruous, then you can clearly see where the disorder comes from. Or, perhaps you are unclear about the real purpose of the room. Examine both your purpose and your activities.
- Remember to include hallways and foyers.

Chapter 4

DE-CLUTTERING THE CHAOS

A peaceful mind is a productive mind.

Once we know the purpose of each room, and which activities we need to accommodate or eliminate, then we may proceed to the next step. We have to de-clutter to put our plan into action. The first law of household organization is to keep it as simple as possible. Less really is more, so we have to concentrate on simplicity. Most of us have acquired more junk, paper, and stuff then we can possibly use in a lifetime. It clutters our lives, gives us more work, and multiplies our cleaning efforts. It begins to stress us and completely overtakes our living space.

All of us recognize that clutter is a deadly vice in our lives; none of us will argue with that assertion. It is just that we don't know how to begin to de-clutter our lives. So let's get to the root of the problem. Much of our clutter is accumulated as a result of fear. We hold onto things because we think we will need them one day. I have worked with clients buried in masses of clothing but afraid to throw any of it away, because they thought that one day, they might need it. Unfortunately, what they could not see was that even if they really needed it one day, they would not be able to locate it because they were buried in clutter.

Fear of deprivation is the first hurdle to be crossed when dealing with clutter. Here is where we must be honest with ourselves. Many people who come from deprived backgrounds will find they are particularly susceptible to fear-based hoarding. Many of the elderly people I work with still hold onto things because they remember when they did not have things. In particular, I have found that those raised during the Great Depression, in low-income households, or in challenging financial situations tend to hold onto things more.

Perhaps, on an unconscious level, they still remember things being rationed from their youth. They fear not having enough. Those images of childhood deprivation need to be acknowledged in order to understand the root of the problem. This is not the only reason people hold onto things. Some elderly people hold onto things because they fear letting go of their youth, or fond family memories. Actually, all clutter has memories attached to it. It is those memories that must be dealt with effectively. We have to admit that, for most of us, clutter is an emotional issue.

Often, we have trouble separating who we are from what we have, so we become attached to anything that enters our homes. Even inanimate objects become our cherished offspring. Perhaps it is part of our depraved nature or human frailty, but we tend to want to hold onto whatever we get in our hands. Thus our homes are full of paper, mementos, and anything that is a testament to where we have been and what we have done. Recognizing this inescapable fact—that we tend to hold onto anything that comes into our possession—should give us insight into how to deal with the clutter in our lives.

Emotional motivation to hoard clutter runs deep, so the only way to effectively rid our lives of clutter is to deal with it immediately. We have to pounce on it before it becomes an emotional issue. Anything that stays with us over time becomes part of us, and we will find it hard to separate from it. Once we understand this fact, it becomes easier to remain organized. I often watch home-improvement television programs that focus on organization. I enjoy watching environments being transformed. However, I am often concerned about these newly organized people, especially the ones with tremendous amounts of clutter.

These shows rarely address how these folks got to the point where their homes were such utter messes that they needed massive makeovers. If they were followed up after a specified time, would they have been able to maintain their clutter-free homes and work areas? I point this out because most people do not recognize the extent of their clutter problem until they are buried in the mess. However, clutter does not happen overnight.

Clutter occurs little by little over time, so we must stop clutter before it infiltrates our homes. Mothers are particularly vulnerable to clutter, because we cherish each little item our angelic tykes give us. Your child makes you a soap dish out of shells one week and a painting the next; before you know it, you have a mass of mementos. This, of course, is multiplied with each child and subsequent school grade, camp experience, and holiday celebration.

Let's face it—we just cannot keep a testament of our children's childhood or their love by saving their stuff. Stuff is just clutter. Sometimes we do not realize that we are trying to hold onto our emotional responses to our children. It is healthy and right to hold onto a few mementos, but it is not emotionally good to hold onto every little item of our offspring's childhoods. We simply must separate our emotions from things. I know that this is easier said than done.

Avoiding the clutches of clutter

We avoid clutter by not getting sentimentally attached to anything. This sounds difficult, but it is not. I often tell my workshop attendees that we must deal with clutter by stopping it before it comes into our homes. Once anything is in our homes, then it is an emotional issue for all of us. None of us are immune to this phenomenon. It is always harder to part with anything that makes its way into our personal space. Therefore, I advise people to think of clutter as an enemy seeking to invade their homes and thwart their productivity. Be mindful of everything—and I do mean everything—that comes into your home. There is no exception to this rule.

You must control the items that enter your home. You may go shopping, attend a birthday party, attend a theater event, or get your mail, and before you realize it, you are surrounded by clutter. Stop clutter before it comes in by recognizing the insidious propensity of clutter to sneak up on you and overtake your home. When you leave your home for any reason, try not to bring things into your house when you return. This may sound ridiculous or impossible at first, but it is rather easy when you give it some thought. Do not take home church bulletins, party favors, theater programs, advertisements, free samples, or anything. They will take space in your home and ultimately reveal their true nature: clutter.

If you need information from a document, record the information in your personal planner, but do not bring home more paper. For instance, I never take a doctor's appointment reminder card. I simply record the date of the follow-up appointment in my planner. Thus, I avoid bringing more paper—no matter how small—into my home.

You have to be vigilant when it comes to paper, because this is the craftiest kind of clutter. It camouflages itself in importance. Remember, if you slip up and somehow it gets in your home, it will be that much harder to get rid of it, because once it is in your home, you are apt to become emotionally attached to it. You will be tempted to think that it has some grave relevance to your life, when in reality, it is just distracting you from the important parts of your life.

Eliminating clutter

Clutter is a real enemy, and you must work hard to eliminate it. It keeps you from attending to what is really important. Clutter control is an ongoing battle we must wage daily. It is more than just keeping clutter at bay. We also must accept the fact that the clutter enemy is very subtle. We have to stay on top of things daily. We have to develop this vigilant mindset to avoid the clutches of clutter. There are some very practical things we can do to avoid clutter. Develop a habit of purging regularly. Purge your closets before you go shopping. I always throw away or give away an article of clothing before I buy anything new. Throw out junk mail right away; it must be gotten rid of immediately. Schedule a "get rid of clutter" day periodically. Go through your pantry and throw out unused food items and donate salvageable ones.

Let's be honest. We have to accept the fact that despite our best efforts, clutter is going to get into our homes. It is therefore imperative that we act on things immediately. Schedule de-cluttering times often and in many different areas of your life and home. All of us have to regularly schedule time to weed out the little imps that may be hiding in our closets, under our beds, or in our cupboards. Understanding how clutter operates will help us to stay organized, because once we recognize it, we can work to eliminate it. Clutter is the chief reason most of us fall off the proverbial organization horse. Once we understand that it is an enemy that must be dealt with daily, we can really conquer it. Some people naturally do this; others, like me, have to learn how to stay organized. It starts with recognizing what clutter really is.

What is clutter?

Clutter can be a vague term. What some people consider clutter, others consider treasure. Clutter really is one of those words with a lot of personal interpretation. This is actually an important point, because in order to stay organized, we must apply everything to ourselves personally. Clutter does have some boundaries in its definition, though. Okay, so here's the Cheryl Carter definition of clutter: clutter is anything in your home without a specific purpose. Just as we purposed every room in our homes, we all have to purpose every item in our homes.

Purpose really drives organization. All the items in your home have purposes, or they should not be there. What are the purposes for the items in your home? Sorry, ladies, but here is where I may be a bit dogmatic. The purpose of every item has to be directly related to your personal goals and those of your family. Remember the mission statement you wrote earlier? I hope you did take the time to write it. Everything in your home should contribute to that mission statement. If it does not, then you have to get rid of it. I know that sounds hard; however, if you really took the time to give thought to your mission statement and repurpose the rooms in your house, your home most likely reflects your mission statement. Therefore, whether you realized it or not, you redesigned your home around the mission statement, even if you did it on an unconscious level.

Continue to build on the concept of purpose. Ask yourself: does this item in my home help or hinder us? Does it help to fulfill our family mission statement? Does it enhance our relationships with one another and our Creator? Be mindful of your initial responses to these questions. Honesty is the core of staying organized; be honest with yourself. Is anything in your home keeping you away from what is really important? If so, it is clutter.

Clutter distracts you from the important and gets you occupied with the unimportant. In the long run, clutter can keep you from your destiny. Your goals, heart's desires, and long-range plans are your destiny, and it is those things you should be engaged in on a daily basis, not wading through clutter. You must take the initiative when purging your clutter. Only you can decide what is worth keeping. Be careful, though, and remember that you tend to be emotionally attached to everything in your home. Thus, you may lie to yourself that everything is important. That is why I had you write your home mission statement before you tackled your clutter. Your home mission statement should provide some barometers, because you have already identified what is important to you.

The other barometer you will be forced to deal with is the space in your home. This reality can be a real kicker, because while I may want my home to be a haven for learning (which I do), I simply cannot accommodate all the books I want, because of space constraints. Too many books will also keep me from focusing on my most cherished areas of reading and curriculum. As a home-schooling mom who is also economically minded, this may mean placing some books that are still useful, but not immediately usable, in storage. I do not like this reality of restriction, but accepting it keeps my home in order.

Be careful not to use storage as an excuse to hold onto items that are really just clutter. Determine the limits even of your storage. Collectible items, such as dated comic books, old coins, baseball cards, and antique dolls that you think may be valuable one day should be stored tightly and securely. There should be a limited amount of space given to these collectible items. I have seen people save items, thinking they were valuable, when they were really just clutter. If you limit the space you give such items, such as a box or another specified storage container, then you will go a long way toward controlling it. I will also presume that no more collectibles will be entering your home. In other words: unless these collectibles are part of a home business, they should not be multiplying almost daily.

You will have to maintain a keen eye on your clutter. Items clearly are clutter if they are not purposeful. It goes without saying that if you have not looked at or worn an article of clothing in two years, it is clutter. Chances are, you won't miss anything you have not looked at in years. This is a hard pill to swallow for mothers. But unless you schedule times of reminiscing regularly, you need to throw out old cards, art projects, and even handmade gifts. You may opt to just keep one sample project per child per school grade. Many mothers also journal about their children as a memento. This is quite a good way of keeping memories, and it takes up less space.

The excellent home

Your aim is to have a home of excellence, and too much stuff gets in the way. Excellence allows you to reach your goals without having your time swallowed up in unimportant pursuits, like constant cleaning or rummaging through clutter. Excellence is not extravagance. Your home should be peaceful, effective, and orderly. Extravagance creates more dusting, vacuuming, polishing, and maintenance. Once more, I remind you to separate yourself from the things in your environment, so that you may connect to the greater purpose of your home. Replay this in your head: less is really more. You simply have to pare down to your necessities to be more purposeful.

If you really find it hard to part with clutter, here is a method to try. Store items in boxes, then label them in durations of three months, six months, nine months, and finally one year. Please, only one box per specified date, or else you will be overwhelmed when it is time to view the contents at the labeled time period. Once the boxes are packed, seal them. Place them in storage or in the garage. On the specified time or date, review the contents of each box. You should record in your planner the dates you will open the boxes to review their contents. Is there anything you missed or needed? If so, take it out. If not, toss the box and all the stuff in it. If you are still sentimental, wait another six months. Repeat the process until you have gotten rid of all your clutter. Remember that in addition to this, you should be fighting to keep clutter out on a daily basis.

You will find it easier to get rid of clutter once it is no longer in your immediate environment, simply because you are no longer emotionally attached to it. The further away from you the clutter is, the easier it is to release it. I once had a client tell me that she stored many papers and magazines in the basement in boxes. She felt she could not live without her old magazine editions. A storm unfortunately flooded her basement and ruined all her magazines, but she realized they really were not that important to her. Remember, clutter seems like it is important, but it only takes up space in your home and your mind.

The ABCs of getting completely clutter-free

Okay, so you are ready to de-clutter your whole home. Begin with the room closest to the entrance door, because this will provide you with lots of positive reinforcement. Visitors are apt to notice the change and compliment you favorably. I encourage you to work in only one room at a time, because your efforts will be focused and effective. You are going to de-clutter the room using what I term the "o'clock method." Stand in the middle of the room. Pretend the entire room is a big clock. Start at twelve o'clock. Do everything at twelve o'clock, then methodically move around the room clockwise, de-cluttering as you go. You should circle the whole room, going high and low to eliminate clutter. Look inside curio drawers, under couches, and on tables. Stay in that area until you have removed all the clutter.

You will also need three large heavy-duty trash bags or boxes. Label them "Throw Away," "Give Away," and "Put Away." The "Throw Away" bag is for all the items that are going straight to the trash. The "Give Away" bag is for those things you are going to give to others or to a charity. Finally, the "Put Away" bag is for items that are not in their proper places. These bags can be placed in the middle of the room, or you can drag them around with you as you "o'clock" the room. If your room has minimal clutter, it is easier to position the bags in the middle of the room. However, if you have a lot of clutter, it is more effective for you to advance the bags along with you as you move about the room.

Keep in mind the uses of the bags. Anything you place in the

"Give Away" bag should have a definite recipient. You might even use Post-It notes if your bag is excessively full. Do not guess who should get which item, because most likely it will end up remaining in your home. If it has no recipient, let's face it: it is trash. In addition, this expends valuable mental energy. Telephone a charity before you start this project, so you will have a pickup or drop-off date to motivate you to complete the task. Remember: if it is junk to you, it probably will be to someone else as well. Throw away the doll with no hair, and the cow cookie jar with one eye missing that goes moo when you open it. Be tenacious and courageous when going through your personal mementos.

The "Throw Away" bag is your most important bag. It should be the most full. Make certain you have more than one "Throw Away" bag—you will need them. If you find that your "Give Away" and "Put Away" bags are filled to capacity, but your "Throw Away" bag is lacking, then you are doing something wrong. Throw away items immediately. Follow your instincts. Do not second-guess yourself; when in doubt, throw it out. If you are thinking, *One day I might need this,* throw it away. "One day" will never come. It is not a purposeful item, because purposeful items are generally used regularly.

The "Put Away" bag is for items that will go in another room. Perhaps you wish to relocate your children's toys as a result of repurposing the room. Place the toys in this bag. I caution you to know exactly where you are going to put these items. Do not just place them in the bag. You may want to have separate bags for certain rooms, or perhaps specified bags of books, toys, clothes, etc. Of course, the severity of your disorganization will determine whether or not you choose to separate the items in each bag.

This may take time. Do not overexert yourself. Give yourself starting and stopping times. Work can expand to fill the time. Therefore, I suggest you allot a certain amount of time to complete the task. A kitchen egg timer works well. Tackle the closets last. Look inside coffee tables, bureaus, and nooks, as well as on exposed shelves. Throw out old pens, faded notes, scrap papers with telephone numbers and no names or notes—you no longer know what they are. You must de-clutter each room before you can clean it or organize it effectively. It is a chore even the most organized person must undertake periodically. I still plan regular times of de-cluttering my home. Think of it as pruning a beautiful plant to make it grow more beautiful.

Another form of de-cluttering that I have encouraged many mothers to use is termed "topical de-cluttering." This form of de-cluttering might be used when you have an abundance of one item taking over every room in your house. For instance, papers, toys, clothes, books, or videos may be gathered from each room in your home, then sorted, purged, and stored. Once again, use the three-bag system. Some items, once gathered, will need to be given away, others put away in suitable storage units, and others thrown away.

Clearly, if items are in every room, they must be purged. Topical de-cluttering is good when you have items that are in almost every room of the house and you cannot figure out a simple way to control them. When our family was moving, I found that topical de-cluttering helped me to purge down to the bare essentials. Once the items are gathered, we put them in categories, so that we can see the categories. Once things are in categories, we can purge the categories and determine our spatial limitations.

Remember, the key to staying free of clutter is to keep things simple. Assign specific places for everything in your household. Everything should have a home, or a place it belongs. Always place items back in their homes. If, by chance, you find your home cluttered for any reason, you can do topical de-cluttering or "o'clock" your rooms. I "o'clock" almost daily to maintain a clutter-free purposeful environment, otherwise I am prone to fall back into bad habits. Once you have de-cluttered, you can clean. In the next chapter we will discuss how to properly and effectively clean.

Keys to Organized Living

- Use a large calendar to record family events.
- Purge frequently.
- Don't be afraid to throw out things.
- Don't take others' junk or unwanted items.
- When in doubt, throw it out.
- Have places for everything.

How long do I keep it?

Three years:
>Medical insurance (in case of disputes), credit card records (if paid off, to prove payment)

Six Years:
>Personal tax records (includes all documentation, such as medical, sales, job expenses, deductible items, and utility receipts,)

Forever:
>Legal documents, birth certificates, death certificates, and all vital documents: passports, licenses, etc.)

Accountants suggest you hold onto all business tax records, including accounting records, incorporation papers, tax forms, etc., indefinitely. You'll need to place such items in an inactive or reference file system.

Online Billing Services

Online bill-paying services are becoming increasingly more popular. They are available at most banks, credit unions, brokerage firms, and financial institutions. I'm a staunch online-billing advocate because it reduces paper clutter.

Advantages

- Convenience: Pay your bill from any computer, whether you

are home or on the road.
- Saves money: No more late payments. You never miss a payment.
- Frees the mind: You can also set up automated payments for repeating bills, such as mortgage, rent, telephone, or other monthly bills.
- Complete record of payment and buying history with the click of a mouse. Includes dates and all vital information.
- Fosters disciplined spending and buying habits, because you can limit the amount you will spend and request.
- Saves time: Spend it with your family.
- Alleviates stress: Stop worrying if the bill arrived.
- Bills are better organized. You can locate them electronically and track your spending in different areas.
- Reduces paperwork: No need to search endlessly for a canceled check. Records are accurate and well-ordered.
- Data can be synchronized to your home accounting or money-management software, such as Microsoft Money or Quicken,
- Most services offer liability for fraud and guarantee there will be no late fees.
- Pay anyone, not just big merchants. Simply indicate payor's name and address, and the check is mailed out.

Chapter 5

CLEANING, FILING, AND SIMPLIFYING—OH MY!

It is easier to obtain something than it is to maintain it.

Once you have de-cluttered, you can clean your home. Many moms think cleaning and organizing are the same thing. Actually, they are not. In fact, many of us try to clean and organize simultaneously, and end up sidetracked, or worse, discouraged. We organize items when we place them back in their correct place or home, thus making the place more functional. We clean or spruce up for hygienic and decorative reasons, thus making the place beautiful.

A mom once told me that she had concentrated so much on organizing that she had neglected the beauty of her home. Everything was functional, but her home was not purposeful, because she wanted her home to be a place the family enjoyed. Instead, her family often flocked to their bedrooms, because the family living spaces were not inviting. It is important for us to balance beauty and function in our homes. When you are simplifying your home, be sure to give attention to the details of beauty.

Cleaning products: what do I need?

Now that you have simplified and organized, it is time for the real work: cleaning. Cleaning involves two distinct elements: maintenance and method. I was not trained in how to clean, so this is an area I had to study in order to get results. The experts or cleaning professionals use specific products—why not use the same for your home? I use janitorial cleaning supplies for all my cleaning chores. In fact, I save money and time by only purchasing them once a year. I purchase them in concentrated form, so they take up very little room in my home.

I use the following products: liquid disinfectant cleanser, heavy-duty cleanser, glass cleanser, shower cleanser, floor cleanser, wood cleanser, furniture polish, floor wax, toilet cleanser, and sealer (for countertops). I also I purchase the following equipment periodically: sponges, pumice stone, white-backed sponges, and air freshener. I also have the following equipment: five spray bottles (*commercial* ones, not the flimsy spray bottles you get at the discount stores), an apron (to wear when you are cleaning and to store items), a cleaning caddy (to keep everything in one place), industrial-strength rubber gloves (for use when cleaning with chemicals), a milk crate (to store cleaning supplies), a lamb's-wool duster (the other kinds only spread the dust around, instead of picking it up), cotton cleaning cloths (or you can use old towels), small dust rags (old towels), a squeegee (for the shower, mirrors, and windows), a quality broom, a sponge mop, and a cloth string mop.

I developed this cleaning-supply list after reading "Is There Life After Housework?" by Don Aslett. Aslett is a professional house-cleaner who places emphasis on buying the right equipment and cleaning products and letting the product do the work for you. A word of caution here; be careful not to use products that are too strong on surfaces. Be sure to read the label and follow directions to the letter. Correct products will reduce the time it takes to do a job. If you really stopped to realize how long it takes to do a chore, you probably would not procrastinate, so getting the right cleaning solution is essential.

We procrastinate doing our household tasks because we magnify the tasks in our minds. Often, I would put off cleaning the bathroom because I thought it would take too long. Most household jobs are done quicker than we think when we employ the right methods. For instance, I found out that the bathroom can be cleaned at least twice a week, and it only requires an average of seven minutes.

You can also put disinfectant wipes in the bathroom and encourage family members to wipe down the counters and fixtures daily, which will make your big cleanups even shorter. You may employ "o'clocking" for cleaning, just as you did for organizing. Start at twelve o'clock and move around the bathroom clockwise. Spray the cleanser, and then wipe counters, the toilet, and the sink. Give the cleaning solutions time to work on their own before you begin wiping. Use a squeegee in the shower. Then work from the top to the bottom: spray mirrors and damp-mop the bathroom floor. This can be done in the average bathroom in about seven minutes.

Bathroom maintenance may be hastened with a diluted solution of disinfectant in the spray bottles in the bathroom. You can also add a bit of baby shampoo to your cleaning solution to make it more effective, because shampoo removes body oil. Generally, our shower stalls get grimy as a result of body oil. I encourage the kids to spray the solution after showers and baths to prevent major grime buildup. The kids are only too happy to spray, because they like to use the spray bottles. Make certain the chemicals are not harsh and do not have a strong odor if you are going to enlist the help of your children.

You may heavily dilute cleaning solutions, since children tend to be quite generous with the cleaning-solution spray bottles. You may have to remind them not to spray it at each other, as well. There are also all-natural alternatives to commercial cleansers. For instance, baking soda is a good abrasive, and vinegar cleans mirrors and windows well, without streaking.

Many rooms in your house can be quickly cleaned. The kitchen is one such room. Counters, tables, the stove, and the sink should be cleaned and cleared every night. I usually use disinfectant cleanser on the counters because of concerns about food poisoning. I use heavy-duty cleanser on the stove, the sink, and most major appliances. Spray all the surfaces. Do the dishes, or load the dishwasher. Wipe surfaces. Reapply cleanser, if necessary. It is really quick when you realize how little there is to do in the kitchen.

Enjoying cleaning

Few of us enjoy cleaning. There are so many more interesting things to do. However, like it or not, it must be done, so we do need to develop a way to make it more enjoyable. You may put on upbeat music—or slow music, if you are the meditative type. I like to listen to a teaching or self-improvement tape. Use an egg timer or an electronic timer to time your cleaning sessions, because that reaffirms that there will be a specified end to your cleaning. Some of us procrastinate because of the time involved, and knowing the end is coming will help us to stay on task. You can also make a game to see how fast you can do a chore. Some enterprising mothers trade household tasks with others—you do someone's windows while they do your floors. Have a house-cleaning party.

Play with your kids while they help you clean. Sometimes I pray, or talk on the telephone using the headset when I clean. Promise yourself a reward after you are finished cleaning. Give your kids an incentive to clean to motivate them to do a good job.

By this point, you should have simplified and gotten rid of

those pesky knickknacks, replacing them with beautiful live plants or something more functional. If you find you are doing a lot of dusting and moving items from place to place, chances are you need to de-clutter a bit more. Always "o'clock" and de-clutter before you begin cleaning. After you have de-cluttered, then you can clean by "o'clocking." You should never try to use the "o'clock" method to de-clutter and clean simultaneously. Always organize first, then de-clutter. Keep a sharp eye for clutter when you are cleaning, because you will delight in shining cherished possessions. If you find that you are frustrated when dusting items, perhaps those things are just clutter in your home. Remember, you "o'clock" a room by circling it methodically, like the hands on a clock.

Daily household tasks

There are some household tasks that must be done daily. They include: making the bed, sorting the mail, washing the dishes, wiping counters, and putting misplaced items away. One of the best ways to reduce cleaning is to prevent the dirt from coming into your home. Most businesses use industrial mats to catch the dirt and grime from people's shoes, and we should too. These mats are made to keep dirt from entering your home. They can be purchased at a hardware, carpet, or cleaning-supply store. Place one inside and outside every entrance of your home. This should reduce vacuuming, because it stops the dirt from coming in.

Cleaning schedules are an individual matter. In the past, I have purchased books with detailed cleaning programs using index cards that I failed to implement. I suggest that you make a list of everything that needs to be done in your home, then make your own schedule. Everyday maintenance is the key to an orderly home, so each day I "o'clock" each room in our home. I go around clockwise and put things in order. I have a lost-and-found box, in which I place everything that is out of place. The kids can retrieve these items by paying a fine (usually a quarter) or by doing extra jobs around the house. Actually, I have had to retrieve some of my own things out of the lost-and-found box too. We need to set examples for our families by submitting to the same rules we give them. The lost-and-found box works for our family because I find that I do less nagging. If someone is missing an item, they assume—rightfully so—that it is in the lost-and-found box.

Remember that our homes should be neat and orderly, not antiseptic. Antiseptic homes are hollow and lifeless. Our homes should be cleaned to be functional places we enjoy, not like sterile hospital rooms. It is better to do a major cleaning in the fall, when our houses tend to be closed up more than in the active spring season. When we clean in the fall, our efforts last longer.

As I have struggled to maintain a household, I have discovered that managing a household involves an understanding of two key elements: inventory and maintenance. Everything we do falls into one of these categories.

Inventory items keep the family moving and spontaneous. These items are generally their essential needs. Most times, these things cannot be delayed. They include food, clean clothes, etc. I have to feed my children. They need to wear clean clothes. I have to pay the electricity bill, because I need lights. These things cannot be delayed. Maintenance items can be delayed. The kitchen floor may be sticky, but the family will still function. Your windows may be full of grime, but you can still see out of them. I don't advocate sticky floors or grimy windows, but I hope you get my point. Inventory items should be taken care of first in your home. This will free you to address maintenance issues.

One important inventory item is the laundry. This is a job with various steps. Often we neglect to think through the whole process, so we do not complete the laundry in a one-time segment. Reduce the steps you take when doing laundry, and you'll see what I mean. I hate doing laundry, so I do it every day. No, it's not some redemptive, character-building spiritual exercise—I simply hate dealing with a large volume of laundry, so I try to do it every day, so it doesn't pile up. With a husband who goes to the gym daily and three active kids, this is actually quite easy for me.

Get help from others. Train little ones to sort the laundry and older ones to help. Teenagers should definitely be doing their own laundry. My kids have their own laundry baskets, so they fold and put away their own clothes. See the laundry chart for suggested ages and responsibilities. You may also put individual family members' socks in mesh laundry bags, which are available in most convenience stores like Wal-Mart or Kmart. By giving family members individual mesh sock bags, you do not have to match family members' socks. You can also pair children, so that the older one trains the younger one how to do laundry. In fact, there will definitely be enough laundry to economically run the washing machine if an older child who is training a younger child does the load with the trainee sibling.

Meal preparation

The other area in the home that is of major concern is meal preparation. This too is a multifaceted task: it involves shopping, planning, preparing, and cooking. The time spent in this area also can be reduced. You should only be going to the grocery store once a week or less. This can easily be accomplished with some planning. First, visit the store you frequent and write down the items in each aisle. Next, type it up, if possible. Photocopy it and write your grocery list on it. This will reduce your shopping time, because you can shop by the aisles and not zigzag when shopping for your family. This speeds up your time in the supermarket and makes it more purposeful.

Menu planning also will save you time, energy, and money. For working moms, there are many great cookbooks with simple meals that do not take long to prepare. Take time every Saturday to plan the next week's meals. I try to plan for two weeks worth of meals. Do not forget the kids' snacks and lunch foods. You can also cook for two weeks, or even a month at a time, if you have the freezer space. Usually I purchase prepared foods when they go on sale. This helps at times. Keep dinnertime as uncomplicated as possible. Opt for simple meals. Prepare a double portion when you do cook and freeze the other half. Reduce stress by deciding beforehand what your family will eat on certain days. You can designate days as Pizza Friday or Hot Dog Thursday. To keep meals healthy, you can make a salad on the side. This reduces the time you are cooking.

Meal preparation does not have to stress parents. Include your kids in meal preparation, so that you can talk to them while cooking. You can include your spouse in meal preparation too. That will allow the whole family to talk with one another. It can really draw a family close together and make cooking less stressful.

Paper management

As I share in my home management workshops, managing the mail was a major issue for my husband and me. Often, when my husband came home from work and wanted to see the mail, I could not find it—generally because I had placed it somewhere out of the reach of the baby. This created frustration and tension for both of us. It was embarrassing, and it was obvious that we needed a mail system. I'm still not sure why it took me so long to realize it, but now I know that every family should have a mail-management system. This system is just a general one. Perhaps you can use it to jumpstart your plan.

As I mentioned earlier, having a system helps keep us organized. Remember to personalize the system. I have used this system for many years. My clients tell me that this mail system helps them even when they do not have the time to file their mail every day because it gives them an anchor to come back to, so they do not get overwhelmed with the mail.

The system is really easy. Get colored folders from an office-supply store or a large convenience store. Most organizing products go on sale right after Christmas, when people are making

New Year resolutions; that is the time I generally replace my worn folders and other materials. Get a package of multicolored folders. Once you have your colored folders, every piece of mail should be placed immediately in one of the following folders, or tossed in the trash immediately! Label your folders like this:

Red:	To Pay
White:	To Do
Yellow:	To Hold
Green:	To File
Blue:	Spouse
Orange:	To Read.

The Red Folder. This is your financial folder and it holds all your bills that need to be paid. A calendar should be placed inside the folder so that you can see when a particular bill is due. Many credit-card companies will change your bill due date to suit your needs. Sometimes knowing all your bills are due on the fifteen of the month reduces your paperwork. There are also online billing companies, which will sufficiently decrease your paperwork and time in paying your bills, so you can do something more important and purposeful.

The White Folder. This folder contains those things on which you will take immediate action. Anything that you must do goes in this folder. These activities still have to be planned. You do not necessarily do what is in your "To Do" folder at the same time you are opening the mail.

The Yellow Folder. This folder is for putting things on hold that you will eventually use, but that do not need to be filed away, such as wedding invitation directions, the trash schedule, etc. This folder should never be very full, because it is transitional material.

The Green Folder. This folder is for all those items that should be filed away at a later date in your household file cabinet. Principality taxes, reference material, and other things that you are eventually going to file should be in this folder.

The Blue Folder. This folder is for correspondence relating to your spouse. Now the mail is in one spot, waiting for him to read it. If your kids are old enough to get their own mail, they should likewise have their own folders.

The Orange Folder. This folder is for any mail that will take over ten minutes to read. I take my reading folder everywhere with me, and in my ongoing battle to defeat clutter, I trash material as soon as I have read it.

Household filing

File papers, don't pile them. Make an immediate decision about every piece of paper that enters your home. We are in an information age, and homes accumulate more paper than ever. Paper is one item that enters a home like a bandit. Perhaps we think we will miss something, and we feel compelled to read every piece of paper that enters our homes. As a writer and an avid reader, I cherish every piece of paper as a prized literary work to enhance my life. I have had to develop the discipline of throwing out paper. It has not always been easy, and I have often found myself poring through piles that I wish I had just thrown away immediately.

Household filing is best done in broad categories, although some people I have worked with prefer the alphabetical system. However, these moms were already well-organized and generally did not want to invest in the time or expense of revamping their existing systems. I point out the fact that there is more than one way to handle files because, as with all organization, you will gravitate to what works best for you. Many household filing systems are more elaborate and complicated than they need to be. These kinds of files are breeding grounds for more unnecessary papers. All filing systems must be purged. Paper is an insidious enemy that tries to sneak in when we are unaware.

To begin the process, get a two- drawer filing cabinet, or file-size boxes, if you prefer. You will probably need to throw away a lot of paper before you start the process of filing. Be careful not to over-organize a filing system. For home filing systems, generalize your categories. For instance, all appliance warranties would be in one file. You want to be able to retrieve a document within a few minutes. You need to take the time to develop a classifying system for your files. Business losses total untold dollars every year because documents are incorrectly filed.

File names should be broad and inclusive. Ideally, use a file cabinet, but if there are spatial limitations or aesthetic considerations, then file boxes may be used. These may be purchased at any good office-supply store. These boxes can be slipped into some inconspicuous place. If you are using a file cabinet, try to utilize hanging files. Your family files should be separate from home-office files. Your files should be broad and inclusive, but you will certainly want separate client files. Remember to be clear and specific. For instance "Old Plans" and "2001 Report" are too vague. Write down specifically what is in each file. Your broad categories may be broken down. For instance, travel may be broken down into travel agents, restaurants, hotels, etc. See a sample of how your filing sheet might look at the end of this chapter.

After you have written down all the categories and identified the section into which each file will be placed, write a master list of the exact name and location of each file. Insert this list in a file in front of all the other files. Place another copy in your "To File" folder, which I will explain to you later. (If you have a desk, place this on your desk; otherwise, hang it on the wall.) This will prove invaluable for keeping your filing system in order. The household file should be arranged in the following order: Household, Family, and Personal. This corresponds to how frequently you will be referring to documents. Most likely, you will be filing and referring to financial documents first, and you may need to occasionally refer to household documents.

Now that your filing system is in order, let's move on. You now have a place to put all that paper. Your self-designed filing system will save you time and effort. In the beginning, be patient with yourself as you set out to change. The basic premise is that this system should be personalized. If you have a family member with a chronic illness, you may need a whole section for medical files. If you are a family working your way out of debt, you may need a whole section dedicated to credit cards, and you may choose to hold onto credit-card receipts.

Your filing system should be quite simple. Each file should be alphabetized under its category. Remember, files should be purged quite regularly. If you are audited, the Internal Revenue Service may require tax records as far back as seven years. Therefore, all household records should be kept for seven years. In my home, I also have an inactive-file box. I file old paycheck stubs, mortgage records, cancelled bank checks, and outdated tax records. Periodically, I will shred these documents, once the statute of limitations runs out. This is done so that the household file does not become cluttered. And never mix home business files with household files. Filing is a boring and tedious job, but it must be done.

Filing our papers, cleaning our environments, and bringing order to our homes certainly streamlines our work. However, we also need to know how to help others to cooperate with us in order to maintain order in our homes. In the next chapter, we will discuss how to help others help us.

Get Off Junk-Mailing Lists

- DMA Mail Preference Service (P.O. Box 9008, Farmingdale, NY 11735-9008)
- Stop Junk Mail Association (800-827-5549)
- Private Citizen (800-CUT-JUNK)
- Consumer Research Institute / Stop the Junk Mail Kit (P.O. Box 612, Ithaca, NY 14851)

Cleaning Schedule

Every day
"O'clock" each room
Wipe kitchen counters and tables
Do dishes (load and unload dishwasher)
Make beds
Assist children with their beds
Sort laundry and do laundry
File mail
Give incentives to kids for completing chores
Spray showers and tubs with cleaning solution
Wipe sinks and counters

Bi-Weekly
Vacuum high-traffic areas
Do laundry
Clean bathrooms (toilet, sink, mirror, floor, etc.)

Weekly
Damp-mop floors
Sweep hardwood floors
Use lamb's-wool duster to lightly dust furniture
Change bed linen
Vacuum indoor and outdoor mats
Get rid of old magazines and other paper items
Clean the exterior of appliances
Clean the interior of microwave

Monthly
Do heavy dusting and polish furniture
Vacuum upholstery and drapes
Clean corners on bare floors and carpets
Re-wax heavy-traffic areas
Clean out refrigerator, stove, and cabinets

Disinfect wastebaskets and trash cans
Wash doormats

Quarterly
Wash windows
Clean garage
Wash patio or deck
Clean and check furnace, air conditioning, etc.
Clean oven
Degrease stove
Vacuum radiators and heat vents
Move furniture and clean under it

Yearly
Strip and re-wax floor
Wash walls
Touch up nicks in paint and repair wallpaper
Clean light fixtures
Wash miniblinds and shades
Shampoo carpets and upholstery
Clean out drains and gutters
Wash aluminum siding
Sweep chimney
Wash ceilings

Chapter 6

MANAGING OURSELVES AND OTHERS

*Children do not do what you expect;
only what you inspect.*

Our lives would be perfect if we could just decide the purpose of each room, de-clutter it, and then clean it. If this was all we had to do, we could merrily ride off into the sunset, knowing our homes would forever be in order. The problem is that we do not live our lives in a vacuum. Effectively managing our kids is part of the process of organizing our lives. Some of us would admit that we first have to manage ourselves.

The key to managing ourselves and maintaining order in our homes is honesty. Honesty, you may remember, is the core of all change. Change only occurs when a person is honest. Honesty with yourself in any area always yields major change. Okay, so if we agree we are going to be honest with one another, then we have to admit when we are wrong. So here it is: while your family may have contributed to the mess, ultimately you were the one with poor home-management skills. This may be a bitter pill to swallow, but the good news is that you can be a catalyst for change.

Most likely, you are well on your way to changing the way you do things in your household and life already. There are going to be definite changes that everyone will see. Congratulations. However, I want to caution you not to expect everyone to jump on the bandwagon with you and to eagerly and enthusiastically embrace your desire for change. To be frank, they probably won't like it. After all, your children are used to things being the way they were when you were flying by the seat of your pants. It is true that they intrinsically crave order, but they are not necessarily looking forward to doing more work. You will need help.

Prayerfully ask the Lord how you should proceed. You may have to get an accountability partner. This person may be your husband, or perhaps another mother. You will especially need a cheerleader on the days you feel like throwing in the towel. Some moms actually have weekly telephone calls or meetings just to cheer one another on. Having someone to speak with also will motivate you to stay on top of things, rather than slipping back to your old ways.

Put it away

The first way you manage yourself is to think like organized people. As a reformed "messy," I recognize that, like many of my clients, I tend to think in a nonlinear way. I am creative, and my thoughts generally bounce all over the place. It is not that I do not want to be organized; it's just that so many other things flood my mind, so organizing always took a backseat to other, more dominant thoughts. I have learned that there are a few basic things that will keep things in our lives in order, and these are my almost-daily reminders.

First, I had to remind myself to put away what I take out. It sounds like a little thing, but most of what we call cleaning in our homes is really just putting things back where they belong. Putting everything in its place also reduces stress and eliminates searching for items that you know you have somewhere in the house. When you use the hammer, put it back in the tool box immediately after use. This sets a good pattern for your children to observe as well. Our children are going to pattern their behaviors after us, so we really have to work hard to remind ourselves of this principle. This is almost so simple that you may be tempted to gloss over it. Putting items back in their appropriate places (or homes) really reduces cleaning and organizing time.

Review your purpose

Next, I remind myself to keep reinforcing the purpose of each room to everyone. Do not violate the purpose of a room, or you will have disorder. If possible, post the purpose of each room where family members can view it. This engenders cooperation, because everyone feels part of the process. Seeing the purpose posted is a constant reminder.

At some point, as you developed the purpose of each room, perhaps you sat down with your children (if they were old enough) and reviewed the purpose of each room with them. You will find that you get more cooperation if they understand why you made certain decisions about your home. This is not to suggest that they will always cooperate with the purpose, but it does offer the possibility that they might understand why they cannot eat potato chips in the den.

Make decisions quickly

As much as possible, handle everything only once. This includes mail, soiled socks, homework, and notes—just about anything. Make decisions on these items quickly. Indecision is the cause of many messes. Organize things at their points of use. If you like to read in your easy chair in the evening, make sure a bookshelf or a basket is nearby. Utilize multiple items when necessary. For instance, make more than one changing station for the baby, if necessary: one upstairs and one downstairs.

Establish house rules and cleaning schedules, and post them. You will get more cooperation if the rules are clear, concise, and posted! If you tend to be messy, you need to raise your standards; if you are too meticulous, you may need to alter your standards so that your home does not become an antiseptic hospital.

Training children and teenagers

Children need four distinct steps in developing household skills. They need steps to be specifically outlined if you are to gain their cooperation. First, demonstrate the skill to the child. Let the child see you making up the bed. This establishes the standard. This generally happens naturally when children are toddlers or preschoolers. They will follow you all over the house, begging to help. Insist that they watch you first; don't just let them delve into a chore. Allow the child to help you make the bed. By participating with you, children try out their skills. This is the time to correct any errors the child may make when performing the task. Finally, supervise the child while he or she is making the bed. Stand silently and watch the child make the bed.

If children make mistakes, then send them back to step one, where they will once again watch you make the bed, then help you make the bed. Finally, assign the task again, and once again watch. After you have determined that the child can manage making the bed, then move to stage four and assign the child the task of making the bed. Once you have assigned a child a task, please be certain to put time in your schedule to periodically check up on the child. The younger children are when this sequence is introduced, the better, because they will cooperate with the process. Although you will see results with children of all ages, clearly younger children are generally eager to progress through the steps, because they want to emulate you.

Teenagers may resist the watching part at first. They may

think it is too babyish, but each step is necessary, and you will avoid frustration later if you follow each step. Teens, of course, will also quickly progress through all the steps. Instruction is important, because many times we tell our children to do things they have not been taught to do. A child's room may look clean to him, but we may find it unsatisfactory. Training them and giving them a standard puts them on the same page with us. Remember, always demonstrate, then let them participate, then supervise, and then assign a household chore.

You can also make a chore chart and give out stars to the children when they complete their jobs. Assign children tasks with their physical, mental, and emotional well-being in mind. Be careful not to push too hard too soon. A child must be emotionally as well as physically able to do a chore. Take time to thoroughly train your children in household tasks. Do not assume they should just know how to do a task. Give teenagers real responsibility. Your house-tending chores should diminish as your children get older.

The atmosphere of your home

Your family or home mission statement should govern every house rule. Be patient with everyone, especially yourself. It takes time to really change, but in the end, it is all worth it. Remember, the most important aspect of your home is unseen by the human eye, but felt deeply by the human heart: it is the atmosphere of your home. Atmosphere is reflected in the way you keep order in your home. You can keep order by love, or by law. When you keep order by law, your home is regimented. Family members keep order out of fear of angry reprisals. Mistakes are not tolerated. There are a lot of rules and regulations to keep everyone in line and the house showroom-perfect. Rules are made to restrict. There is a strong authoritarian spirit in this kind of home. The home is clean, yet antiseptic. In short, this home is clean, sterile, and cold!

On the other hand, when you keep order by love, your home is orderly, friendly, and very comfortable. Most things are in place, with an occasional mess here and there. The rules and regulations are there to maintain the peace. The rules are based on collective understanding, and are viewed as a means of protection for everyone. Family members' mistakes are not met with angry reprisals, but as opportunities to grow more responsible. A strong sense of team spirit is felt. This home is neat and comfortable. It is warm and endearing.

Ultimately, the spiritual atmosphere in your home governs the physical atmosphere. Our homes can be very legalistic, ruled by law and enforced by anger and punishment. Or your home can be ordered by love and enforced by caring for one another. The characteristics of your home should always be considered. A busy home with five small children may look different than an empty-nester home. As mothers, we should try to understand child development and set realistic and reasonable expectations for our children. Be careful not to be too lenient, though. A child also needs to develop responsibility skills. In everything, we should avoid excesses.

Remember accommodation and elimination

Always consider your family's needs. Remember accommodation and elimination when keeping order in your home. Consider accommodating the shoes on the living room floor with a fancy plant-rack for their storage place. A quilt-cover rack may be necessary in the bedroom, to deal with clothes that used to be tossed on the floor. A box in the living room also works well to deal with daily messes; items that do not belong there may be tossed in the catch-all box to keep the room orderly. This helps us to stay organized. Have a realistic standard of cleanliness. Consider your family's characteristics and activity level when determining your level of cleanliness. Whenever you notice a mess in a room or a space, ask yourself the purpose of the space. Is someone violating its purpose, or do you need to reassess its purpose? To stay organized, you have to keep asking yourself why messes are occurring.

Be creative

Storage space is a major issue in growing families. Consider all your options for increasing storage space before you move or do a major home renovation. Perhaps you can store stuff under items in your home. You can purchase elevating bed coasters, which allow for higher storage under the bed. You can also use these coasters with certain types of sofas. Look for creative ways to store things; do not think in the typical way. Hanging shoe bags are excellent for storing small toys, scarves, and many different kinds of accessories. You can also hang things from the ceiling. Hanging plant holders in the kitchen can store weighty fruit or other heavy items. Think very nontraditionally. Store items on doors, in drawers, and almost any place you find room.

Assess your storage needs before you buy organization products. Too often, people see sales featuring organizing products and buy them, only to realize they will not work for them, because the products do not address the issues that caused disorder. For instance, I once went to a friend's home office to help her organize it. She complained that she did not have any desk space because her desk was so small, yet she had many desk organizers that were taking up room. When I suggested that she get vertical organizers and use her wall space, it was as though a light bulb went on. She had never considered that keeping the desk completely clear was what spurred her productivity.

Think of creative ways to deal with clutter, so that you are not exerting a lot of mental, physical, or emotional energy on little things that really do not matter. As I mentioned earlier, our lost-and-found box was initially implemented simply because I did not like reminding the kids to pick up their stuff. Anything left out of place or that violated the purpose of a room was placed into the lost-and-found box. I did not nag or complain; I simply placed it in the box. The kids had to pay money to retrieve their belongings.

Over the years, this idea has evolved, and we have upped the ante. Each night I "o'clock" the rooms and place items in the lost-

and-found box. Items can only be retrieved once a week, so I am not constantly going back and forth to the box. The box is stored out of the family's immediate view. Our family is on an honor system. We do not lock up our box, but some mothers who have implemented this idea have told me that it only works if they lock or hide the box. Prayerfully consider what will work best for your family.

We also have a family game box, because we lost parts of board games or found it difficult to store all the small pieces. Routinely, we place our board games in a plastic container. Game pieces are stored in sealed plastic bags. In my home, game boxes tend to get destroyed quickly. We tend to play a lot of board games, since television is not really an option in our home.

We also have a small "I don't know" box. This box contains small gadgets and items that may be valuable, but cannot be identified. I place the kids' little doodads and my husband's gadgets in it. If they are not claimed by a specified time, they are tossed in the garage. The box is easier than trying to figure out where something belongs when I am "o'clocking" a room. It has also stopped me throwing out important screws, nails, and other objects that belong to my fix-it-up husband.

Family rules and scheduling

State family rules in the affirmative, not the negative, for instance, "In this family, we put away what we take out." Family rules should be posted at all times where everyone can see them. Reward your children for keeping the home clean and organized. Plan special meals, like a pizza-party night for everyone. Do not be critical. If you do say anything critical, make it a point to say at least three positive things.

Time management is a family issue. A family calendar is a necessity. List kids' scouting meetings, recitals, plays, trips, etc. Put down your commitments too. Everyone should use the family calendar. You can refer to it before you make a commitment. It also helps to slow down the pace of family life a bit. You can put in family meetings, special dinners, and other events that you want all of the family to attend. Calendars are great! A calendar is a necessity for all busy mothers.

You should also have your own personal calendar and make appointments with yourself. These appointments can be for personal development, spiritual growth, or anything. Either way, post them so family members will know you are unavailable at these times. You need to make the time to fill yourself up before you pour into others. Women in particular spend much time pouring into the lives of others, yet very little time filling themselves back up.

Family communication center

You can also reduce a lot of stress by having a family bulletin board or communication center. I have one in the kitchen. You need someplace where your kids can put permission slips and other things that require your signature. You can use a horizontal file folder, or cover a cereal box with contact paper. Train your children to put notes in the box. This way, you can read them at your leisure, and not when you are cooking dinner or otherwise occupied. Our communication center has also been used as a place to put encouraging notes to other family members. You can also have a suggestion box, where kids and adults can add their ideas about how the family can effectively function. A calendar should be near the family communication center.

Checklists

Checklists are great. One mom I know not only has lists for everything she does, but has laminated them, so will always have them. Lists in general are great. I have morning personal-hygiene checklists for my children's morning routine. We have church checklists, to ensure we get out in a timely matter. We also have bedtime checklists. They have become a real lifeline for us. They also help us not to forget things. Checklists are great because they relieve stress. I have helped mothers write morning, traveling, and afternoon checklists. Checklists also create routine.

Post checklists throughout the house, so that children will not forget routines. Checklists help children to anticipate events. You are apt to get more cooperation when children know specifically what is expected of them. I have found that my clients with attention-deficient disorder really appreciate checklists. It relieves them of the pressure of trying to recall everything, and it has the added bonus of subconsciously developing a sense of structure. Checklists are fairly simple to make: you simply list everything you have to do, in order. See our checklists at the end of this chapter.

Children and time

Children see time differently than we do. They unashamedly live in the present. This is a very delightful aspect about children. However, for many of us busy moms, it can become an annoyance. It is not that we want to rob our children of their childhoods. We just want them to move along a little more quickly and be more cooperative with us, especially when we have to get so many things done. I have found that children do not necessarily understand time as we do. They need to understand that time has boundaries. I have found that an electronic countdown timer works wonders, because children can see the minutes clicking and ticking away.

The visual nature of the timer helps them to understand that time is an entity that is moving along. Checklists with time constraints will also help children who tend to be dawdlers. Simply post the allotted time that you would like a child to complete a task. Be sensitive when making choosing your time intervals, as you do not want to make your child neurotic and unnecessarily rushed.

Your children will cooperate with your organizing efforts if you make it easy for them to perform chores. Put clothing hooks at their eye level. Adjust your standards, and reward them for their efforts. Assign tasks to them that they are able to do according to their ages and developmental and emotional abilities. Even if they can not complete a whole chore, break it down into steps of things they are able to do. See the laundry chart for different facets of doing the laundry—even toddlers can be trained to do some portion of the laundry.

This breakdown can be done with almost any chore. Think about the other family chores that you might typically only think of assigning to teenagers. There probably is a small incremental step that younger children can do. Can you see how even small children can take part of activities such as meal preparation and cleaning? By assigning chores in this way, children will naturally grow into taking over the task, without much resistance.

Our children can do more than we think. Even small children can put away their own clothes. You can label dresser drawers with pictures for children who cannot yet read. We use Fun Tack. It was originally used by school teachers to post educational charts and signs on their classroom walls without harming the paint. We use it because it does not harm the finish on our wooden bureaus. Fun Tack is adhesive that looks remarkably like chewing gum. It is quite sticky. I have used it to attach pictures on my children's bureaus so that they remember to place their clothes in the appropriate drawers. You can use magazine cutouts if you are not artistically inclined.

Be mindful that since Fun Tack looks like chewing gum, small children may try to eat it. Fun Tack may be found in office-supply stores, teacher stores, or mainstream book or educational stores. Do a Web search on it if you really want to find a store near you that sells it.

Getting out of the house in the morning

Getting out the house in the morning is the number-one issue for moms. Some of us cannot even get to church without a major emotional upset in the family. It does not give our children the sense that their Lord Jesus is lovingly patient and kind when we are hurtling threats at them to move faster, eat quicker, and get themselves dressed. This is the start of the day and the week, and it serves your family best if everyone can be at peace. It has to be pleasant, because it sets the tone for the whole week. This is best accomplished by creating a morning checklist for young children. You can also create a Saturday evening checklist. For now, let's concentrate on your morning checklist. It can be simple.

Sunday Morning Checklist

- Brush your teeth.
- Wash your face.
- Get dressed.
- Make your bed.
- Pray.

Children can place stickers near each item they complete. This reduces the possibility of you repeating yourself and becoming the family nag. Children like to collect stickers. You can reward them for full sticker charts at the end of the week. These charts can be posted on their bedroom or closet doors, or on the bathroom door.

For infants and toddlers, dress them and put them in a safe spot, like a high chair where they can eat Cheerios. You may want to try placing them in a playpen with a video or a few preschool toys. (For those inevitable spills, always have a second set of clothing on hand).

To get children to move more quickly, give them their own alarm clocks. My son had his first one when he was just six years old. It was great. There are many benefits. Younger children will strengthen their number-recognition skills. They will also develop a concept of time; the sooner this skill is developed, the better. Youngsters are more responsible when they are more aware of the time.

Older children can learn to be more responsible by getting themselves up and out of bed in the morning. The sooner responsibility is learned, the better. A parent should not be waking up a preadolescent in the morning. It is their responsibility to get up on time. You may need to allow some children to suffer the natural consequences of consistently getting up late. This may include not eating breakfast, or "missing the bus" (my husband's term for the family car) and walking to church.

We have to be aware of time. Time is the one commodity of which we do not get any extra. You can make more money, but once you have spent your time, you do not get it back. Teach the importance of time, utilizing a simple kitchen timer. A timer has many uses. You can also use a timer to make almost any activity a game. Who can be the first one down to breakfast? Set the timer. Pancakes can also be a wonderful motivator on busy mornings. You can buy the frozen variety, or double your recipes on Saturday, freeze the remainder, and pop it in the microwave during the week. The key is for you to be prepared every morning.

Prepare as much as you can the night before. Lunches should be packed, if you are to be in church for a long time. Sunday-school bags should be near the door. This will ease your stress and make the mornings more peaceful. This way, mornings will be peaceful and memorable for the whole family.

You should do something significant before all the family members begin to leave. My family gathers together, stands in a circle, and prays for one another. It is a really positive way to start our day. It also builds strong family ties.

As we learn to manage ourselves, we realize that it is our time that must be managed in order to help our family members succeed. In the next chapter, we will discuss how to plan our days so that we are more productive and efficient.

Tips to set the atmosphere in your home:

- Have a realistic standard of cleanliness. Consider your family's characteristics and activity level when determining your level of cleanliness.
- Develop a family mission statement that draws family members together, beyond just the physical upkeep of the house.
- Plan times of family games and other activities in your home, so that it is a fun place to be for the entire family.
- Share your family mission statement with all family members. Brainstorm any changes together.
- Plan regular times of hospitality. Your house should not be a museum, but a haven of happiness to be shared with all. Set dates, so you do not procrastinate about having people over. You should have people over several times a year.
- Instead of nagging, just state what you see, in a matter-of-fact way, when the offender is within earshot. For instance, "I see red socks on the kitchen floor."
- State family rules in the affirmative, not the negative. For instance, "In this family, we put away what we take out."
- Understand the emotional climate of your home. When things seem rather tense, examine your attitude and relax some rules.
- Plan special meals like a pizza-party night for everyone keeping the house neat.
- Do not be critical. If you do say anything critical to a family member, make it a point to say at least three positive things.

The Laundry-Sequencing Chart

Task	Suggested Age	Ability	Able to Perform
Awareness of dirty clothes	18 months–4 years old	Fine-motor skills beginning to develop; emotionally able to be aware of need to pick up clothes	
Pick up clothes and put them in hamper	18 months–4 years old	Ability to grasp clothes and place them in designated place for dirty laundry	
Sort clothing into lights and darks	3.5–6 years old	Child must recognize colors and nuances in clothing	
Select water temperature and press appropriate buttons	2–10 years old (with parental assistance and complete supervision) 11+ (once child has been trained	Fine-motor skill to press buttons and understanding of water-temperature cause and effect	
Measure detergent and add additives when needed (bleach, fabric softener, etc.)	12+ years old Be careful: in addition to bleach fumes being toxic, detergents can be dangerous.	Ability to measure and the maturity to be cautious around toxic substances. Ability to lock up detergents to keep from younger siblings.	
Time the cycle and remove clothes	12–15 with parental reminders 16+ independently	Ability to plan time to return to task of completing the laundry	
Place in dryer or hang-dry clothes	10–15 with parental reminders and verbal and visual instruction 13+ independently	Ability to follow directions and follow visual and/or verbal instructions	
Sort and fold clothes	5+ years old	Ability to recognize different kinds of clothes and family members' clothing.	

Chore List for Various Ages

Two–Six Years
Pick up their toys
Sort silverware
Put their clothes in labeled dresser drawers
Help sort laundry
Wipe down dinner/breakfast table
Wipe baseboards
Pull up covers on their crib/toddler bed
Help load the dishwasher
Set the table
Weed the yard
Water plants
Use non-toxic spray cleaner in the bathroom and kitchen
Daily use of disinfectant wipes in the bathroom
Empty wastebaskets
Use a handheld vacuum cleaner

Seven–Twelve Years
All of the above and:
Wash and dry dishes
Rake leaves
Assist in snow-shoveling
Unload dishwasher
Damp-mop floors
Vacuum floors
Care for pets
Make simple microwave meals
Wipe counters
Wipe down walls using non-toxic cleanser
Clean outdoor furniture
Assist in preparing family meals
Make their own beds
Clean their own rooms

Organize their own toys
Take telephone messages
Do household filing
Assist in mowing the lawn
Dust furniture
Make shopping list
Put away groceries
Weed garden
Plant flowers in the yard
Wash siding
Make their own lunches
Wash the car
Help care for family pet
Sort mail
Organize family cassette tapes,
Organize compact disks
Organize videocassette tapes
Clean windowsills
Water lawn
Take out garbage

Thirteen–Eighteen Years
All of the above and:
Prepare family meals
Go grocery-shopping
Scrub the bathroom
Wax floors
Mow the lawn
Use the trimmer and cut hedges
Care for younger siblings
Clean the garage
Tutor siblings
Take care of family pet
Organize family files

Organize family library/books
Work as a secretary or receptionist in your home business
Wash blinds
Clean out refrigerator
Do their own laundry
Train younger siblings in household tasks
Polish furniture
Help plan the family budget
Chauffeur younger siblings to activities
Run errands for family

Eighteen Plus
All of the above
Plus rent!

Chapter 7

DAILY PLANNING

Time management is really choice management.

The final phase to living a life of meaning and purpose is execution, or daily planning, so let's get right into it. You should purchase an inexpensive planner with month-at-a-glance and week-at-a-glance views. It should be rather compact, so you can take it everywhere. Some people prefer the ease of new electronic organizers, in which they can store all the information in one place. I have used an electronic PDA (personal data assistant) such as Palm One, but I find that since I am a visual person, I need the tangibility of my paper planner, although I do enjoy the portability of my PDA.

I strongly advocate weekly planning, because it gives you an excellent opportunity to get an overview of your week. Sit down, preferably on Sunday evening, and plan out your week. You should review your personal mission statement, goals, and family commitments. I also enjoy reading my Sunday-sermon notes on Sunday, because often I like to integrate spiritual goals throughout my week. I also write down things I would like to do for people and schedule them in my calendar. I schedule little things like calling friends and doing projects with my kids. I also record precisely when I will follow through on promises I have made to my family and friends.

Once I wanted to put an "I love you" note in my son's lunchbox. The mornings were always so hectic, and in the evenings, when I made his lunch, he was always around. So I plugged writing the letter into my schedule while waiting for his bus. When he arrived, I immediately took his lunchbox and discreetly placed the note inside it. The next day, he was surprised and thrilled! All it took was a moment of planning and thinking. Sometimes we get so frazzled that we find we have no time to think, and we miss precious moments like that. I think it is important that we regularly schedule thoughtful moments for ourselves and our families.

Weekly planning may seem a bit taxing when you first embark on the practice, but you will find it will help you to stay organized. It helps your time to remain more purposeful, because you can focus on your long-term goals. Hopefully, you will take the time to write out some goals for yourself. Moms are notorious for helping everybody else with their goals, but not making their own goals. Make goals in these key areas: Financial, Physical, Mental, Family, Professional, Social, and Spiritual. Your goals should be value-centered; that is, they should reflect the things most important to you. What kind of house would you like to live in? What kind of job would you like to have? What kind of salary would you like to make? What would you like to see for your family?

Set goals

Look at the goal worksheet at the end of the chapter. Brainstorm about what your life might be like in the above areas. Ask yourself why you want to achieve your goals. Why you desire to achieve your goal is generally more important than the goal itself. Many people set goals but do not achieve them, because they are trying to work on too many goals at one time. After you make a list of your wants and why you want them, cross out the ones that can be delayed. By choosing to pursue one goal in each category, you become laser-like in your life. The sharper your focus, the more potent and purposeful your life will be.

You should check your goals annually. Remember, a goal without a deadline is just a fantasy. You may want to stagger the dates of your goals so that you do not impose unnecessary internal pressure on yourself to achieve all your goals at the same time. Goals should be broken down into manageable parts. After you write a goal, you should then write out the steps to get you there. Ideally, you should be working on your goals every day, if only for a brief time. It is the consistency at which you pursue your goal that makes the difference.

Turn all your long-term goals into short-term goals. Please do not neglect the process of actually writing down your goals, because writing them down brings clarity and purpose. All your goals should then be broken down into precise, tangible tasks. See the following example:

Long-term goal: To become a college professor
Short-term goal: To go back to graduate school

Your weekly tasks might include:
- Requesting applications
- Studying for the GRE
- Researching programs
- Working out a financial plan to pay tuition

Remember that ideally, you should be working toward your long-term goals daily. In the above example, the major goal is broken down, so that almost every day, this mom is pressing toward her goal of becoming a college professor. This may involve you just doing a little bit each day. If you are unable to work on each goal daily, do not be overly concerned, as long as you are progressing weekly. Also, be aware that you may not be able to completely plan out every item in your week, because motherhood itself carries a certain degree of unpredictability.

Weekly planning still gives you the edge, though, even if you cannot be assured of everything that will happen to you. Weekly planning does not mean that you abandon daily planning. The two should be done in tandem. It still may be necessary to plan some portions of your day on a daily basis. My husband generally will plan the following workday before he leaves work. He says that this eliminates taking the office home with him. We all appreciate that!

Organize your day

There are basically two ways to organize your day. The first is most applicable to entrepreneurs and stay-at-home moms. I refer to it as "division time organization." I list the different divisions of my life, or my roles. Then I list the things I have to do under each category. (See below.)

<u>Wife</u>
1. Rent movie for Derek
2. Call Derek at work to say thank you
3. Pray for Derek's meeting with director

<u>Mother</u>
1. Write note for girls' dance teacher
2. Play Memory Match with kids
3. Write in kids' journal
4. Read sewing and woodworking books
5. Quiet time with kids

<u>Family Manager</u>
1. Cook dinner
2. Take out summer clothes
3. Update bill system

Home Educator
1. Review new curriculum
2. Locate new LEAH group
3. Order Elijah Company books

Writer
Read *Writer's Digest* magazine

Professional Organizer
Return telephone calls
Outline new manual

Woman
Quiet time
Exercise

Notice that in each category I listed everything I had to do for that day. In this way, I can analyze in what divisions I am falling short if I fail to achieve all my daily tasks. My daily tasks and goals are related to my long-term goals. This works for the entrepreneur as well. Consider one day of my scheduling:

Marketing
1. Research magazine readership
2. Bookmark sites
3. Update marketing plan

Human Resources
Schedule assistants for May seminar
Write job descriptions for future positions

Administrative
1. Return telephone calls
2. Fill daily booklet orders

3. Order more envelopes
4. Renew NCCA membership

<u>Planning</u>
1. Outline new book
2. Schedule time with Cynthia

If you are a home businessperson, you can see in what ways your day's energy is being directed. Sometimes, when working at home, it is hard to see where your business and home time is being divided. When I first began scheduling like this, I noticed that I was unlikely to accomplish my marketing tasks. Actually, I was unconsciously procrastinating. This schedule allowed me to realize in what area I was procrastinating. It also helped me to locate the black holes in my scheduling. I was able to correct my mistakes immediately. Now I am aware that I need to work more diligently on my marketing tasks. This scheduling method really causes you to target your day.

The other way to organize your day is rather traditional. You simply list everything you have to do, and categorize tasks by level of importance:

1. Must do
2. Should do
3. Could do

Tackle the "must-do" items first; check off each item as you do it. Remember, as a result of your weekly planning, some fixed activities should already have been plugged into your day. These items should always be "must-do" items. Thoughtful moments should always be "must-do" items. Remember, thoughtful moments usually do not take long. It is because they seem so small and inconsequential that we often delay them, waiting for the perfect moment, which rarely occurs.

Self-evaluation

Another key to daily planning is self-evaluation of your daily activities. This is necessary to monitor your progress. You can approach it in two ways. One way is to keep a journal. You need to ask yourself key questions. Did I achieve my goals this week? Remember to make adjustments after you evaluate your day. Know yourself! Are you a morning person or a night person? What motivates you? Also consider your personal and professional responsibilities when planning. Do not attend three stress-filled meetings on the same day you volunteer to help your daughter's Girl Scout troop.

You must have personal development and planning time *every day*. This is non-negotiable. If you do not make time to plan, then you plan to fail. You can get this time by rising early, staying up late, or taking less time at lunch. It is extremely important. Personal daily evaluation is the best place to begin. Take the time now to plan your week! Schedule a time when you will regularly engage in weekly planning.

When you schedule different activities in your day, estimate the time it will take you to complete the activity, and plan accordingly. This is important, because we often over-plan our days due to unrealistic expectations. Begin to estimate the time it takes you to get projects done. For instance, doing the laundry involves many facets and probably takes longer than you are aware that it does. Attempt to overestimate the time when you first begin this process.

Example:
<u>Family Manager</u>
Laundry (1.5 hours)
Grocery shopping (1 hour and 45 minutes)
Reorganize closets (2.5 hours)

You should plan your day the night before, keeping in mind

that your weekly schedule acts as a blueprint for how you want your week to progress. For example, if you want to get some reading time in the evening, it may require you to make certain the kids are in bed by a specified time, which may require you to schedule dinner or other activities earlier.

Reduce stress

Think about your typical schedule. Visually walk through your day and identify the areas of stress or frustration. Think of creative ways to alleviate the stress. For example, if your morning routine is stressful, brainstorm—with your family—creative ways to get rid of the stress. You might want to try a morning checklist to relieve the stress and get cooperation.

Remember always to be honest with yourself. Ask yourself, "Did I accomplish all I needed to do today?" and "What can I do differently to be more productive tomorrow?" The answers to these questions should be brief and should be written right in your planner book.

The following are general keys for mastering your day and achieving maximum productivity. They are self-explanatory. Be physically prepared for the day. Get up early. Studies indicate that you think more clearly in the morning than at any other time of day. This should be the time you handle your most tedious tasks. The morning also sets the tone for the day. Make certain your mornings are peaceful.

Prepare in the evening for the morning. Set the breakfast table before you go to bed. Take out your clothes, including all accessories. Plan to eat a healthy breakfast. Breakfast really is the most important meal of the day. It gives you the energy to handle your day.

Do everything possible to make certain you are in top physical condition. Get an annual physical. A desire for an inordinate amount of sleep coupled with a lack of enthusiasm may indicate a form of depression. A lack of energy may suggest you are anemic or have an iron deficiency. You may need extra vitamins or supplements. Practical physical concerns should always be addressed before you demand more from your time.

Appreciate the time you do have to be productive. You actually have more time than you think. Make use of *all* available time. Use small segments of time. Generally, I read the mail while waiting for my computer to boot up, instead of exasperating the computer and myself by unnecessarily slamming the keyboard. Instead of waiting to have five hours available to clean the garage, begin to do it daily in fifteen-minute segments. Small segments of time can really add up!

Your thoughts are significant too. When you are overwhelmed, think more futuristically and not just in the present moment. The present moment limits your perspective. Your present circumstances do not dictate your future. I knew when I was home with my kids that I was destined to help people organize their lives. As a result, I was able to enjoy the days, which seemed full of pouring juice, wiping noses, and changing diapers, knowing that my influence did not stop there. This positive perspective enabled me to cherish the time I had with my children. I enjoyed them as a natural part of my life, not an interruption to my plans. Motherhood is a high calling, and we owe our children and our mates the best.

Making good plans

Our plans are based on our thoughts and formed by our words. Watch the words you speak to yourself. We tend to believe what we hear over and over again. When you make a mistake, do you tend to say "I was so stupid to do that" or "I never do anything right"? You will begin to believe you are stupid or that you will never do anything right. As a result, you will be thwarting your own productivity. Listening to yourself is a key to personal productivity.

Planning is another key to being more productive. In the planning stage, we can pre-live a day and determine how it will be—

what we will do, where we will go, who we will see—with very few surprises. Visualize how you want your day to evolve, knowing that man makes his plans but that your steps will be directed by the scope of your day.

Plan flexible time. Remember the relationships that are important to you. Look at your goals and consider your values in your planning. Never forsake relationships for resources.

The essentials

Planning for each day is important. A daily planner or organizer is essential. It will keep you on top of things. It also trains others to respect your time. They will know their requests will be given careful thought. Generally, I consult my calendar before I say yes to anything. Others have come to expect this of me, and usually do not expect an immediate response from me.

Never take on another commitment without consulting your weekly and monthly calendars first. You cannot make a decision based solely on your daily calendar, because you need to get the big picture. If you are out every evening except Thursday, then you should not commit to do anything on Thursday just because you have it free. You probably need a quiet evening at home.

Quiet evenings are important, because you usually prepare for the next day in the evening. Therefore, you should guard your preparation time. Look at your goals and consider what you need to accomplish each day. Be certain not to schedule a lot of activities just because you can fit them in your calendar, thereby neglecting your planning time or goals. Most importantly, remember to schedule meaningful moments in your daily schedule.

Meaningful moments are vital, because they feed our relationships. Relationships give sustenance to our lives. A woman in my former church will often send me an encouraging card—just letting me know she is thinking of me. It always arrives at just the right time. Her investment of ten minutes makes a tremendous deposit in my life. Surely, each of us has at least ten minutes to make a difference in someone's life.

Generally, meaningful moments are things we want to do for others, but we never quite get around to doing them. Take the time to send a card to someone. It may be advantageous to purchase a box of all-occasion cards, so you will have one when you need one. Schedule time to talk with friends as often as possible, so that you can to maintain and enjoy the relationship. Go out to lunch with a co-worker. Let other people know they are important to you.

This concept can be very significant with your children. We tend to blow off our children's requests because we are not "in the mood" or "in the right state of mind" to do something. What we really mean is that we did not plan for it. This can be remedied by actually planning to do fun and memorable things on a regular basis with our kids. Plan to take them out for ice cream, do an art project, or bake them cookies. You will be amazed at how simple, little things mean so much to others.

Time Chart: Please record an average day in increments of fifteen minutes.

Time   Activity

List at least nine things you have been meaning to do in the "meaningful moments" chart that follows, and note when you will be able to do them. The moments are probably very small in duration.

1 _____
_____

2 _____
_____

3 _____
_____

4 _____
_____

5 _____
_____

6 _____
_____

7 _____
_____

8 _____
_____

9 _____
_____

Choose some goals and list the reasons you want to do achieve them and the reasons you may not want to achieve them (or in other words, why you may be procrastinating).

Goal   Why I want to achieve   Why I may not want
         the goal   to achieve the goal

Long-Term Goals (with deadlines):

Financial: _____
_____

Physical: _____
_____

Mental: _____
_____

Family: _____
_____

Professional: _____
_____

Social: _____
_____

Spiritual: _____
_____

Chapter 8

DEALING WITH PROCRASTINATION

You get more out your time by investing more in yourself.

Procrastination

Procrastination is a serious issue in time management. There are various reasons people procrastinate. Most of us have put off something at least once in our lives. The results of procrastination are obvious: missed opportunities, lost income, and damaged relationships. The reasons for procrastination are not quite as obvious as the results.

Most procrastinators really regret their inaction, yet they continue to procrastinate. It is a paradox of sorts. This is because procrastination is more than just putting off an unpleasant task. On one hand you want to do something; at the same time, you do not want to do it. It is real inner conflict.

This conflict occurs when you have valid reasons to want to do something, but also reservations about doing it. The valid reasons occur on a conscious level, but the reservations are generally on an unconscious level. The conflict is so intense that you just put off doing a task. In this way, you do not deal with the issues at hand.

Procrastination on this level generally occurs over long periods of time. It usually relates to major tasks. The best way to deal with this kind of procrastination is to ask yourself why you do not want to do something. Be careful not to just give surface answers. Probe deeply. Address the reasons why you do not want to do something.

Ask yourself why you want to do something, then ask yourself why you really do not want to do it. Generally, the excuses you give for delaying the task will reveal the reasons you don't want to do it. Be careful, though—they may just be excuses masking the real reasons why you do not start or complete a task. See the example below of a woman who delayed painting her garden gate.

Task: Painting the garden gate

<u>Why I want to do it</u>
1) It *should* be done.
2) I should finish what I start.
3) It looks bad when we have company.

<u>Why I don't want to do it</u>
1) I don't like painting.
2) I don't think about it until I see it.
3) I have more important things to do.

This person really has no desire to paint the gate. Clearly, she sees external forces at work. She feels that she "should" do it. It is not the result of her internal motivation, but rather an imposed demand to do it. She may also be unconsciously rebelling against authority, because she feels that she has to do it. Notice that she does not think about it until she sees it. It is not important to her, yet for some reason, she feels compelled to paint the gate. This is the conflict. She needs to recognize this and decide she wants to do it for herself if she is to finally tackle the task.

Your language reveals the reasons for your procrastination. Whenever you find yourself saying, "I should ___," you probably are reacting to an external stress, as opposed to a personal motivation.

Procrastination is not always so indirect. This method of examining the reasons you want and don't want to do a task works quite well nonetheless. You can look at things on a weekly or monthly basis. Ask yourself why you have not done what you said you would do. Sometimes it is not internal conflict, but external conflict. See the example below of the woman who wants to go to the gym. Notice her reasons for wanting to go to the gym clearly outnumber her excuses. Below, she examines her excuses for a month.

<u>Why I want to go the gym regularly</u>
1) To stay in shape
2) To feel better about myself
3) To stay healthy
4) Better appearance
5) To lose weight
6) To look better in clothes
7) I already paid for it
8) To have more energy

<u>Why I have not gone to the gym (excuses)</u>
1) Can't find a good time to go
2) Need to go to bed early to go in the morning
3) Helping kids with homework
4) PTA project
5) Tim worked late a lot

In this case, there is no inner conflict; it is a scheduling issue. Notice that Tim (her husband), the kids, and the PTA take precedence over her going to the gym. In this case, her procrastination is the result of not planning a precise time to go to the gym and communicating this to others. While all her reasons for going are valid, she is not precise in her goals. She should turn all her wants into specific goals, for instance: to lose fifteen pounds by next month at the rate of three pounds a week. This would motivate her to go to the gym weekly.

I encourage wives to share their goals with their husbands. Generally, my husband and I will sit down together Sunday evening, review our week, and discuss our weekly goals. In this way we become one another's accountability partners. During the week, I will inquire about how he is progressing toward his goals. He does the same for me. As a result of this practice, it is very difficult for me to procrastinate. An accountability partner is important. Choose someone to talk to about your goals and plans. Hold one another accountable.

Another reason you may procrastinate is because you lie to placate yourself. I do this sometimes when I have a sink full of dirty dishes. I tell myself I will wash them later, usually after I rest awhile. I do this rather than deal with the fact that I have allowed the dishes to pile up—or, more to the point, that I need to develop a positive habit so the dishes do not pile up. I do not have to deal with the issue at that moment when I lie to myself. When I decided to be real with myself, I developed a positive habit to deal with the dishes.

Positive habits can really prevent procrastination. It takes about twenty-one days to fully form a new habit. Positive habits and personal planning will eradicate most procrastination. Identify the habits you want to develop, then work toward developing them.

Approach all change in your life methodically. Break large,

overwhelming tasks down into small, manageable parts. You should break a goal into daily tasks. It is easy to accomplish daily tasks. It is human nature to gravitate towards the easy. We are apt to do the easy, so make it easy to do.

Essentially, procrastination involves moving toward the pleasurable. Build a system of rewards for yourself. For each step you make toward your goals, reward yourself. I reward myself with chocolate-chip cookies when I finish typing a chapter. It is rather ironic that I like to write, but I do not like to type. Therefore, I set a typing goal daily, and only when I have completed that goal do I have any cookies. I have shared my goal with my family, so I cannot ignore it.

Your goals should be clear and measurable. Often, procrastination is a result of just being too vague in defining what you want to accomplish. Be careful not to be so precise that perfection paralyzes you. Perfectionists have a subtle fear that they are not good enough in performing the task at hand. When you find you do not start a task because you do not have the very best tools, the best resources, or perfect timing, you are probably being a perfectionist. You should just start where you are.

The key to overcoming procrastination is just starting where you are. The hardest part about completing a task is starting it. Generally, if you can start, the hardest part is over. So go for it!

Quiet time

Daily success is determined by the quality of our quiet time. Quiet time is the most valuable time, because it is where we get the intangibles that we pour into others. Essentially, quiet time is eternal time.

In quiet time you gain keen perspectives on the intricate details of your day. There is nothing you cannot handle. You get filled with patience and understanding, and respond to the challenges in your day accordingly. Once you have had time to fill yourself up, then you can respond to your children, your husband, and your co-workers out of your spiritual overflow.

When we are short-tempered or short on patience, we are usually short of quiet time. Quiet time secures us emotionally. We are much more productive after quiet time, because we can go about our day in peace. Peace is the prerequisite for productivity.

Quiet time also develops us mentally, because it is a time for purposeful thinking. Mothers with small children really appreciate and need times of contemplation. Quiet time helps us respond to crisis (which will surely come) with calm and resolve. It prepares us for our day.

In my quiet time, I build a relationship with my Creator, God. I have read many books and heard many sermons, but by far, my greatest spiritual growth has been the result of spending personal time with God. It is a time when I am most intimate with my Lord Jesus. I could not live without it! Sadly, this is the most neglected discipline in so many lives. The reasons for this are varied. A major reason this occurs is because most people expect their quiet time to be easy. They fail to plan for it. While quiet time is beneficial and pleasurable, the path to getting there is not easy. It takes planning.

Planning begins long before your allotted quiet-time period actually starts. It should be given careful thought. You should first decide where you will have it. At one point, we actually had a quiet room in our home, where everyone could have quiet time. We merely had to be aware of one another's schedules. Recently, we have had to be more creative. If you do not have a room, then designate a specific place where you will have quiet time every day in the same place.

The consistency of the location is important. Every time you go there, you will be conditioned to tuning out all distractions. You will find that most distractions diminish as you continue quiet time regularly. Some women use a kitchen table, or sit outside on the porch; whatever location you choose, be certain you will not be disturbed.

Early morning is the best time for quiet time, for many reasons. Most family members are still asleep, and you are unlikely to be interrupted. It also sets the tone of your day. Mothers with young children who may not be sleeping completely through the night may alter this a bit. These moms may find it better to have quiet time in the evenings. This time is essential, so use the morning for a brief quiet time and to refresh yourself before serving your family for the day.

The tools you use during quiet time should always be together. I once used a large basket for my quiet-time material. I put my bibles, concordance, journal, notepad, facial tissues, devotion book, and planner in it. You can place your own special books in a basket. I took the basket to a quiet part of the house, so as not to wake others. Although I did not have one specific place to use, I did have very specific materials. The basket really helped to bring a sense of consistency to my quiet time.

Besides the right tools, preparation needs to be done prior to your quiet time. Set out the materials. Prepare the environment. It is hard to have quiet time in a messy room, because clutter will distract you. Ready yourself for quiet time. Open your quiet-time devotional book to the chapter you will read the next day. Glance at the chapter or verse you intend to read or meditate; this prepares you. Also, you should not have quiet time in a room which is typically noisy. Go to a quiet place. Be aware of the atmosphere in your home, and choose wisely.

Quiet time is a personal discipline. You should set a specific goal for it. Make it precise and exact. A vague goal fuels additional procrastination, because you do not have a clear target at which to aim. There are many advantages of quiet time. Decide for yourself what you want to get out of your quiet time. Quiet time is more effective, when you are personally motivated. Share your personal revelations with others. Get a nice journal book, and use it. Be certain that your quiet times can be your most creative and enjoyable times.

The final way you can be more productive is to guard your peace. This can be done by checking the stress in your life; make certain your activities and values are one. Deal with any disharmony in your marriage or other close relationships. Talk things out. Do not deny your feelings; deal with them. Get counseling, if necessary. If you are distracted with other things that bother you, then you simply cannot be at peace. Peace is a prerequisite for productivity.

Relationships and time

Relationships take time to develop, and time spent nurturing relationships is never wasted time. I recall one gentleman who had set an admirable goal. He wanted to build a practice and retire by the time he was fifty. He felt that by retiring so young, he would have unlimited time to spend with his wife and children.

In order to reach his goal, he worked twelve-hour shifts, and all day Saturday. On Sundays, he was exhausted and had no energy left to give his family. His practice did grow, but his wife and children grew to resent him. They hated his long hours and his lethargic disposition on Sundays, when he was with them. In the end, he was divorced and estranged from his children, because he had never taken the time to build a relationship with them when they were younger.

Relationships need nurturing to thrive and are based on love. Love is measured by the time and attention you give to the relationship. Your children want your time and undivided attention. Children spell love with the letters T-I-M-E. Children need it to know that they are important in your life. Your spouse needs it as well. It is a genuine *need,* not just a want. Wants can be delayed; however, needs must be met.

Look at your roles in life. Who you are to others? Examine your goals. Notice how your goals and roles affect one another. In fact, your relationships may be the motivation to achieve your goals. Life is about relating to others. Look at the different roles you play for others (parent, spouse, scout leader, baseball coach, CEO). It is awesome to think of the many roles we play.

A major key to living a life of purpose and meaning is not just looking at your current role, but translating a goal into a future role. You have to see the future before you can experience it. It is really a powerful principle. For instance, I once spoke with a kindergarten teacher with aspirations to be a principal. I encouraged her to begin to think like a principal would think, because you will always move in the direction of your dominant thoughts. I furthered encouraged her to pursue some portion of that goal daily.

When you begin to see yourself differently, others will be forced to see you differently. This principle is particularly applicable to stay-at-home moms, who often feel trapped in the mountain of diapers and car pools. Every week, you should sit down and write down the most significant thing you can do for your relationships. For instance, it may be just sending a thank-you card to an employee or a simple appreciation card to an employer. It is little things like that—the good intentions—that really need to be actualized in our lives.

These thoughtful gestures take so little time, yet can mean so much. My mother often used to remark that she only spoke to me if she called me first, so I made calling her a weekly goal for my role as daughter. She is happy now that I make time for her, and I no longer feel stressed with guilt over forgetting to call her. I used to stagger the time I called her so she was not aware of my scheduling. Well, now she knows, because I have shared this illustration so many times.

Remember in Chapter One when I discussed the importance of relationship time management? Well, this is one way to integrate time and relationships—simply by making time to do small significant and meaningful things. Most of us appreciate the same things, like being remembered on our birthdays, getting a thank-you card, or simply being hugged. Putting small things like that on our to-do lists will yield hefty heavenly rewards, and those things do not necessarily take a lot of time, either.

Think of at least five of your roles. Write them down, from the most important to the least important, and next to each role write something meaningful you can do to enhance that relationship this week. If you do not know what would mean the most, simply ask. Once, I was trying to think of something special to do for my husband. When I could not think of anything, I just asked him. It seems that week was a particularly stressful one, and he just needed my understanding that his schedule would be rather hectic. I gladly obliged, and we both ended up having a great week. Meaningful deeds should be done daily, but weekly is a great place to start. The small investment in time really makes the difference.

Tips to overcoming procrastination
- Set a deadline.
- Share your deadline with others.
- Do the unpleasant things first. Harness the ability to complete a task by visualizing its end.
- Form positive habits. Write down which habits you need to develop.
- Play "beat the clock" with yourself. (Use a timer.)
- Break tasks down into manageable parts.

Chapter 9

PRODUCTIVITY BOOSTERS

An accomplished goal is a gift I give myself.

Productivity is no great secret. It is just doing things more efficiently. Try these productivity boosters—these are proven ways to keep us at maximum efficiency.

Multitask

Most of us already know or instinctually practice multitasking to some degree. We naturally do one, two, three or more things at a time. For instance, you might clear off your desk while speaking on the telephone. I love speaking on the telephone while doing a boring or tedious household chore. However, there is a danger in attempting to do too much. We can burn ourselves out trying to be "superwomen." Thus, while I advocate multitasking, I generally recommend that it be done in scheduled, short periods of time, and not as a major lifestyle choice. Sometimes we do too much, and it breeds an adrenal rush that keeps us moving forward, even when it is physically taxing our bodies. You can pair positive, enriching activities with dull, rudimentary, or boring tasks. This will motivate you to complete a task. Make use of all your idle time; while waiting in line, read a book or make a list. Use your traveling time to listen to a teaching or self-improvement tape.

Get up early

Studies show that working one half-hour in the morning is equivalent to staying up three hours at night. I know this is hard to do especially for mothers with young children, but it has been proven that early morning is "prime time." You will find this great for achieving your goals and catching up on things you thought you would not have time to do. I find that I think more clearly in the morning. I know there are some people who insist they are night owls. I used to be one, but I have found that I accomplish so much more when I wake up early. You do not need a long block of time. A simple half-hour a day yields three and a half hours extra each week. More importantly, you will find that half an hour in the morning, when you are clear-headed, will benefit you a lot more than burning the midnight oil.

Guard your personal-development time

Schedule, in your calendar, a monthly meeting with yourself. Do not break your appointment. It is a very important meeting. You should also plan an extended yearly meeting. At these times, take time to review your goals. When working on your goals, be honest with yourself if you notice that you need to revise your goals. Goals should be made with some level of personal reflection. They are best done away from the hustle and bustle of others. If you cannot get away, then take advantage of early morning and late night, when the house is quiet.

The goal-making process is a very important activity. We tend to walk in the direction of our goals, so our goals can determine our lives. It has been said we tend to move in the direction of our most dominant thought; therefore, our goals must really be something we want to live and die to achieve. Sometimes, in your zeal to make a goal, you may find that you have adopted a goal that you are not really passionate about. Do not be afraid to discard it.

Remember to make relationship planning part of your personal goal-planning time. Disharmony consumes time and energy, so we should work on our relationships. Deal with procrastination in your planning time. Follow your instincts.

Many people set goals but do not achieve them because they are trying to work on too many goals at one time. After you make a list of your wants and why you want them, cross out the ones that can be delayed. By choosing to pursue one goal in each category, you become laser-like in your life. The sharper your focus, the more potent your life will be.

You should check your goals annually. Remember a goal without a deadline is just a fantasy. You may want to stagger the dates of your goals so that you do not impose unnecessary internal pressure on yourself to achieve your goals. Goals should be broken down into manageable parts. After you write a goal you should then write out the steps to get you there. Ideally you should be working on your goals everyday if only for a brief time. It is the consistency at which you pursue your goal, which makes the difference.

Daily planning

Daily planning is the key to long-term success. Writing down everything also helps you to deal with mental clutter. Do not let indecision paralyze you. Keep moving! When working for an important cause or investing in a relationship, do not be bullied out of doing what you know is the right thing to do. Particularly guard your planning and personal time. Always evaluate, and be ready to make appropriate changes in your daily schedule.

Remove the word "try" from your vocabulary. "Try" implies failure and doubt. Boldly declare what you will accomplish each day. When you get up in the morning, speak to yourself, declaring it will be a good day. It has been proven that our bodies naturally follow what we tell them. If we are positive, we draw positive circumstances to us; if we are negative, then we attract the negative, In the Hebrew book of Proverbs, it states that as a man or woman thinks, so she or he becomes. Our thoughts can hamper our days.

As moms, the most critical thing we can do is to invest in ourselves. At times, we can be too sacrificial, to our own detriment. We have to constantly make the right decisions, even in little things, like what we will eat. Most sickness is diet-related; therefore we should snack on healthy things and lead a healthy lifestyle of exercise. A simple thing like increasing our water intake can do wonders for our well-being. In fact, the brain is mainly water, and neurologists suggest that increased water intake will improve brain function.

Be mindful of the time-stealers. Sometimes it is little, insidious things like television-watching. Turn off the television immediately once you have reached the allotted time you promised yourself you would watch television. To really be aware of your time-stealers, write out what you think would be a perfect day. Well, a perfectly scheduled day, that is. What would be your ideal waking time? What activities would you accomplish?

This exercise will help you see where your time is really going and where you want it to go. See the chart on your perfect day at the end of this chapter. Contrast and compare it to how you are currently spending your time. Notice the times in your day when you are doing the same things and schedule similar activities together. For instance, perhaps you can cook all your meals at once. Occasionally, when I prepare a hot breakfast for the kids before home-school, I will start dinner too; this way, at the dinner hour, I am not rushed to quickly prepare everything.

Learn to say no without guilt

Mothers sometimes are afraid to say no. I have found it easier to say no by saying yes. If I have goals and important deadline items in my schedule, I am less apt to say yes to anything. I have also learned the power of a quick no and a slow yes. When someone asks me anything, I am prone to say no first, but sometimes with a qualifier that I will think about it. Actually, I have said this so often that many friends know that my immediate response will be no. We should give our time and talents to those things we are passionate about, but sometimes we moms are hogtied into doing things we really have no personal wish to see to fruition.

Purge items regularly

Purge all items that tend to accumulate regularly. Do not allow inventory items like clothes undermine your organization efforts. Stay organized by regularly purging your closets. Many professional organizers tell us that we wear only twenty percent of our clothes eighty percent of the time; therefore, we really can pare down our closets. Tackle your closet before you do your kids' clothes. The same principle applies to children's clothing that applies to ours.

Go through your closet. In most closets are three kinds of clothing: "where I used to be," "where I'm going," and "where I am." Translation: items that are too small, things you want to fit into one day, and clothing you are able to wear now. Toss out old, worn clothing and give away new clothes that you bought on impulse, but will never wear. Make it a practice to throw away or give away an article of clothing every time you add a new item to your wardrobe. You should consider purchasing a closet organizer. Before you do anything, I must reiterate this point: prune your closets. Do not use your organizer as a way to just store your clutter.

Most closet problems stem from overcrowding. I prefer to hang my clothes in complete outfits. It eliminates a lot of the decision-making process for me. In other words I put my blouse, skirt, and jacket on the same hanger. Some advocate that you hang all blouses together, all skirts together, etc. You get the picture. If you have a lot of coordinating pieces and like to match and explore different colors, this may be for you.

But be careful—are you holding on to a purple fur skirt, just because it might possibly, one day...snow a lot? If you regard any article of clothing with the preface "maybe one day," chances are "one day" will never come.

I recommend that you get rid of wire hangers and just use the plastic tubular hangers, because the clothes do not get tangled. If you like, you can color-code your closet. You know: all casual wear on yellow hangers, dresses on blue, and so on.

A word about accessories: you need to be tenacious in regard to these items. I recommend that you get a belt rack or a tie rack, which you can purchase from almost any hardware store. You can use it to store your scarves, ties, belts, and other accessories. I also recommend plastic shoeboxes with snap-on lids for smaller items. (The snap-on lid is important if the box falls in the closet.) Hatboxes should be used to store hats. If you have a lot of hats, then print the hat type in bold print on the box, so you will know which hat it is without making a mess in the closet.

By all means, keep the closet floor as clean and clear as possible. Hang up clothes that fall right away. The items in a closet are for regular use, not just for storage. In other words, the prom dress you just cannot part with should not be taking up space in your main closet. (It can be put in storage.)

You will also find that most clothing that is contributing to clutter in your home is the result of indecision. When my kids did not have a definite place to hang their coats, there was a tendency for the coats to be all over the place. They did not know where to put the coats.

A laundry day is generally the best day to prune your closet, because your favorite items are likely to be in the laundry. Take everything out your closet and see what you really have in there. Then put all your clothes in categories, or different purposes. Do you have some clothes for formal wear? Church clothes? Work clothes? If you have a large accumulation, clean one closet at a time. By the way, toss out any wire hangers, as they tend to get twisted and leave lines on many clothes. Opt instead to get plastic, wood, or tubular hangers. They protect clothing better than the wire ones. Your may also purchase hangers that enable you to hang multiple items on one hanger.

Personal organizing center

Every mother should have a personal organizing center where notes are placed, meals are planned, and personal and family planning takes place. If you have the space for an office, this is ideal. However, if you do not you have one, remember that you can still make yourself a portable home-organizing center. Get a small container with a lid, or a file box. You can pick this up at almost any office-supply store. You will want to put in it a calendar, a planner, and a folder for notes. Some mothers like to make their mail system part of their home-organizing center.

I hope you also created some checklists that relate to your regular family activities. As I mentioned earlier, they may be laminated. As my children get older, I like to keep them on file, rather than posted throughout the house. Remember, checklists are good to use when you notice any area of your life that is stressing you because things are being forgotten, or when you simply have an extremely full calendar.

You also may also want to include an electronic timer. I use my timer to limit the amount of time I speak on the telephone, de-clutter a space, or work on a project. At times, I can become too absorbed in what I am doing, so I require an external reminder to stop. Our family timer does overtime, because we all use it. Get a good model.

Your personal organizing office will ensure that organization remains at the forefront of your family's schedule. This will really help you stay organized. It also provides one place for all your organizing tools, so they will not be misplaced. Some may laugh, but there is nothing more frustrating than losing your organizing tools. Also, if you establish an organizing center with other mothers, you can continually add to your arsenal and always be getting better at everything you do.

Your personal organizing center will also help you to implement regular cleanups and purpose checkups. We really must regularly assess how our organizing efforts are going to stay organized. A large calendar is a necessity for scheduling and posting personal purpose and organizing checkup times. To stay organized, we should schedule these times, because life happens to us all, and clutter tends to be very crafty. Therefore, we should designate certain days for cleaning. Keep a calendar posted, but also keep a copy in your personal organizing center.

A large family calendar should be posted in the kitchen. You can place important dates and appointments on the calendar. Everyone should use it to post their schedules. Talk with your husband. Set up regular routines. Determine together the positive habits you want your children to develop. Routines done over and over become habits. Remember, habits take time to form—some say at least twenty-one days. Determine the needs of your family and figure out routines that will help form good habits. Target the behaviors most important to you. For instance, if you want your children to make their beds in the morning, establish a routine that will render that result. Use your organizing center as the hub for making these goals.

If you are blessed to have a desk to use as your organizing center, please be careful not to let it become cluttered and unmanageable. Divide the desk into quadrants, and determine the purpose of each portion of your desk. Do not let it just become a dumping ground for all your papers. Piles of papers that cannot be purposefully retrieved are merely organized chaos. You should have a large desk calendar atop your desk to help keep your desk clear. You will find that you think better when working at a clean desk. Place items you use regularly within arm's reach on your desk. A tickler file may be useful to help you keep up with everything.

Tickler file

A tickler file is an organized way to hold onto information and monitor your schedule. It is very easy to make a tickler-file system. To set up a tickler file, number a set of manila folders 1 through 31. Each file should be assigned a single number. Next, get twelve more folders and label them with the months of the year: January through December. I prefer to write the numbers in black, but I write the months in red Magic Marker. Place items in the months you will need them. Then rotate the monthly labeled folders to the front of the files regularly.

This system is relatively simple and often used by busy executives, but easily adapted for home use. For instance, if you plan to attend a convention in May, but receive the confirmation material in September, simply drop it in the May folder. When May arrives, take the confirmation out of the May folder and place it in the folder corresponding to the exact date. Admittedly, a tickler is not for all families, but if you find your schedule is practically hectic, with a lot of sporting, drama, or academic events, this may be just what you need. It is also an excellent place to store airline tickets, doctor-appointment referrals, invitations, and annual maintenance records.

Master schedule

While I do not advocate being a tyrant to a schedule, I do encourage mothers to write down an ideal schedule, then use it to make a realistic master schedule. Schedules help us to get more done and provide a structure for small children. I actually plan my day in segments. My early-morning time is when I have my devotional (or quiet) time with the Lord. Early morning to mid-afternoon is when I home-school the kids. The late afternoon is when I do household chores and volunteer work with our home-school support group. Although I don't engage in volunteer work daily, I do designate this as the time I return calls and do community outreach and relational activities like writing cards or calling friends. In the evening, I generally plan different activities and then schedule each time slot accordingly. I am not tied to my schedule all the time. Of course, on some days I home-school all day or do other fun or deadline activities.

This type of scheduling keeps me somewhat balanced in the different areas of my life. Schedules are not necessarily restrictive, if you realize that they are relationship-driven. I actually schedule time to speak with my husband. We are more apt to find time when it is scheduled. Also, since at times I can be a Type A person, I find that I have to plan time for fun with the kids, and family downtime. Your organizing center is the place to keep your planner, goals, and personal growth information. You should have goals in these key areas:

- Financial: includes savings, investments, and spending habits
- Physical: includes health, diet, and personal grooming
- Mental: includes intellect, reading, increasing concentration, etc.
- Family: includes relationships with children, husband, grandchildren, in-laws
- Professional: includes vocation, career, and job skills
- Social: includes community, church, civic, volunteer
- Spiritual: includes bible-reading, prayer, biblical meditation, intimacy with God

Having a personal organizing center will also keep you focused on making organization the means to an end, and not the end itself, as we have discussed in an earlier chapter. You can formulate your values into a definitive life mission and purpose statement and write it out and put it in your personal organizing center, where you can view it regularly. You may not want your personal information posted all over your home, where strangers and visitors might see it, but you still need it readily accessible, to encourage and inspire yourself to good works.

Writing a personal mission and purpose statement will make daily living choices much easier. It alleviates stress, because it allows you to make sure your activities and personal mission statement line up with one another. There may be many different ways to get to somewhere, but like Alice in Wonderland surmised after her discourse with the Cheshire Cat if she did not know where she was going any path would do. We need clarity.

The first step to achieving clarity is to write your own personal mission statement. Your mission statement should be concise and clear. You should be able to refer to it often, and it should be motivating to you. Ask yourself the questions, "Why do I exist? What contributions do I make to my community, society, and the world at large?" Be specific. Do not just say, "I help people." What kind of people do you help? How do you help these people? Why do you feel so strongly about helping these people?

For instance, the mission statement for my seminar "Organize Your Life" is: *To demonstrate to people the power of a belief system becoming a lifestyle, through publications, tapes, seminars, workshops, and training classes.*

It is something I review before I accept a speaking engagement or teach a class. I make sure that I can fulfill my mission. This helps greatly. Even when business is slow, I refuse to violate my own personal mission by accepting an assignment where I would not be able to fulfill my mission.

Your personal mission is just that: personal. It applies specifically to you and is unique to your personality, temperament, and desires. Think of it like a flame. It illuminates your life. It was ignited in your past, flickers in your present, and is glaring in your future. Think about your present. What do you find yourself thinking about often? How do you see yourself in the future?

Your life mission will evolve over time. It is a process you will revisit time and time again, so do not get paralyzed in the process. God will guide you in this process. But God cannot direct your steps if you are not in the process of moving. My personal mission or purpose has been refined and narrowed as a result of prayer, meditation, bible study, and life experiences. This has taken a number of years. Remember that this is a process that will keep evolving.

Ask yourself when you stand before the Lord, and he says, "Well done, my good and faithful servant." What specifically would he thank you for? Be exact. Think about the talents he gave you. Are you burying them, or planting them in the soil of this life to yield a crop of contribution? If you have difficulty identifying your talents, ask some of your close friends who walk with the Lord. Your purpose is what you think about, desire, and are passionate about. With this in mind, write out your personal mission or purpose. You may need to take time to pray about it. If nothing comes to mind, do not agonize over it; simply move on and revisit the thought at another time, because it will reveal itself more clearly as time goes on. This is an individual activity where there is no right or wrong response. Indeed, it is a personal exercise.

<u>Example</u>: *To lead people to meaningful, fulfilled lives, personally and professionally.*

You may want to write out your values. Your values will become your personal creed. Ask yourself what is most important to you, and why it is important. You may wish to write it in the first person.

For example:

I, Cheryl Carter, value truth above all else. I will be truthful in my relationships, including those with my husband, children, and customers. I will be honest in business dealing and I will be truthful to myself in overcoming my character weaknesses.

Family

I value my family above everything else and will give to them the first fruits of my time, mental and emotional energy, resources, and creativity.

I value my husband's opinion over that of every other person and respect his position as the God-ordained "servant-leader" of our family.

Write out your values in the space below. You can list it or write it in your own style.

1 _____
_____

2 _____
_____

3 _____
_____

4 _____
_____

5 _____

Turn these values into a personal creed. For example: *I value my children, therefore I will spend quality time with them every day.*

I _____ value _____
therefore I will _____.

Design a perfect day in the space below. Then compare it to your typical days. What do you need to change?

Time	Activity

Chapter 10

QUICK SOLUTIONS TO COMMON PROBLEMS

Your home should serve you. You should not serve it.

You will need to survey every room in your home to stay organized. Here is a rudimentary look at the basics of what must be done in each room.

Finding more space

Space can be found in our homes if we get creative with our vertical space. Try to hang up as many items as possible. You may also use hanging plant holders, which tend to be stronger, to store fruit or even moderately heavy home-school supplies—especially those items you want to keep out of reach of little ones. Hanging shoe bags are also excellent for storing small items such as office supplies, sewing doodads, or collectible toys. You can also purchase collapsible hanging filing systems that may be posted over doors. You can also install shelves. Post as many things as possible on the walls and doors.

You can also store things underneath furniture. Under-bed storage units are popular and easy to find. You can double your under-bed storage by placing your beds on coasters. They are available at Bed Bath & Beyond and a few organizing specialty stores. These coasters lift the bed off the floor, so you can store a great deal of clothing under it. You can purchase them in wood or heavy-duty multicolored plastic, which is perfect for a child's room. You can also make them on your own. These coasters may also be used with sofas.

Kitchen

Start with the counters. Your counters should be as clear as possible. If necessary, invest in over-the-counter appliances, or just remove some of the kitchen appliances from the counters. How many times do you really use that popcorn maker, the electric mixer, or the automatic juicer you brought two years ago when you decided you needed to eat more healthily?

Throw away or give away items you no longer need. Be honest and ruthless with yourself. You can find space for the items you still use in the cabinets or other wasted spots. You will find that clean, clear counters will yield the most remarkable results in your kitchen.

Throw away rarely used and unused pots and pans. Basically, you only need one really good, versatile set; this will eliminate effort and time as well as save space in your kitchen. Many times, we just have too many pots—again, guard against sentimental attachments. Give them to a good charity.

Throw away the Tupperware and Rubbermaid. The Tupperware ladies might not like this, but often people have more storage items than they can possibly use in a lifetime. If you feel you simply cannot live without buying a new piece, then throw away or give away the former pieces, instead of adding to your collection.

Throw away or give away those duplicate or triplicate utensils, and you only need a certain amount of dishes and glasses. Many charities can use your old dishes and glasses. Keep the top of your refrigerator clear, unless you have items neatly organized there. Above all else, the only things that should be on your table are a tablecloth, placemats, napkins and the salt and pepper shakers. Store all old recipes in a binder. If you have exposed shelving, keep it as neat as possible.

Linoleum makes an excellent lifetime shelf liner. You can buy it quite cheaply from a hardware store. You will also have to get a cutter. Simply measure it out, and you will never have to line shelves again. It makes cleanups a breeze; just wipe out spills. Remember the purpose of your kitchen. Magazines, mail, and other paper do not belong in the kitchen—that is, unless it is specified in the personal purpose of your kitchen.

You may need an overflow box in the kitchen if you have very little counter space. In fact, if you have a small kitchen, this might be very wise to do, because the kitchen will look cleaner and bigger when the counters are free. Be certain to place frequently used items in your immediate reach. You can also hang pots and pans to give you more counter space.

Living room

This room has to be warm and inviting, because it is usually the first room people see when they enter your home. The living room gives them a feeling for the whole house. You will never get a second chance to make a first impression, so this room may require a bit more attention than the other rooms in your home. Try to set up your living room with clear floor space. Get rid of overly extravagant items.

Collectibles tend to gravitate to the living room. You should only be cleaning things you really love. If you are constantly dusting an old knickknack Aunt Mae gave you but you do not like, then get rid of it. It may be causing you more emotional upset than you are consciously aware of when dusting.

Window treatments should not be too elaborate. Clean out coffee tables and bureau drawers. You will probably have to throw away most of the contents of these drawers. Store meaningful things attuned to the room's purpose even in the interior drawers and shelves. This is where you have to be hard with yourself. Once art is hung on the wall, the remainder may have to be given away, or if not, displayed somewhere else in the home.

Clean off shelves, wall units, curio cabinets, etc. Disperse the contents of the interiors of furniture. Even a beautiful curio can be cluttered with too much stuff, so much so that its beauty cannot be appreciated. Be creative with storage. An ottoman can double as a storage unit.

Keep your living room from becoming the dreaded drop-off zone by remembering the principles of accommodation and elimination. Accommodate shoes, coats, or other items that may be left in this area by making space for them. Eliminate areas where sporting gear or other items are carelessly tossed.

Bedroom

Go through you dresser drawers. Throw out clothes that are too big, too small, or too worn. Throw out old makeup. Don't forget to throw away the costume jewelry and the accessories you have had since the 1960s. Consider—only if necessary—investing in a quilt holder or a chair to put clothes on when you or your spouse comes home tired. This is a personal issue of elimination or accommodation.

The bedroom tends to be a place for more than one activity, perhaps because it is your personal space. Make sure to clean off your desk. Figure out if you need a space for your books, a place to exercise, or a place for prayer, and then change your room around accordingly. Clean out nightstands. Keep your bureau tops as clear as possible. Throw away dusty flowers, old mementos, etc.

To keep your bedroom clean, be certain to always make the bed. When your bed is made, it makes the whole room look better. Always pick up items on the floor. The cleaner and clearer the floor of any room is, the neater and bigger the room appears. For children, you may direct them to first pick up all their toys, then pick up paper, and finally clothes. Those are the items typically found in children's bedrooms. By giving the child one type of item at a time, she or he is able to concentrate fully on picking up the items and is not overwhelmed.

Once your child picks up each item, help him or her put them into categories, so that you both can determine what needs to be thrown away and what needs to be put away. You can use the three bags ("Throw Away," "Put Away," and "Give Away") with each item category. You should also enjoin your child to clean his or her desktop regularly. Be certain that students' desks are adequately lighted, so they will be motivated to do their schoolwork at their desks.

Try to think like a child when scoping out your child's bedroom. Also check the closets. Little ones have a way of using the closets as a catch-all for all their clutter. Make it so that kids can maintain it their own living spaces by putting in eye-level hooks and easy toy storage. Toy boxes are not necessarily the best solution, because they frustrate young children. They have to expend effort and energy just to get a favorite toy that might be at the bottom of the pile. Before you throw away a child's toy, take it away to see if he or she really misses the item. I have been surprised at the toys my children cherished, even though they did not play with them regularly. Rotate toys so they always seem fresh and new to children. I have taken birthday and Christmas presents and hidden them from my kids for a time, so that they would not be overwhelmed with too many playthings at one time.

Dining room

Do not crowd the china cabinet, inside or out. Use items. Not everything should be an ornament. Even fine china is meant to be used. Keep tables clear. It is a table, not a desk. Get a portable card table if you want a temporary desk. This will force you to remove items on a daily basis. Try hard not to let your dining-room table become a drop-off place for junk. Place on it a lovely accent piece, something you enjoy looking at. It will motivate you not to crowd the table.

Bathroom

Clean out the medicine cabinet. Unless you have a major medical issue you may use your medicine cabinet for storage. Toss out expired medicine, old prescriptions, and medications your children have outgrown. My youngest was a preschooler when I went through my medicine cabinet only to find that I still had infant pain-reliever drops and unused prenatal vitamins.

Keep counters clear and clean. Like the kitchen, the bathroom appears bigger and cleaner when the counters are clean. If your bathroom is small, use the wall space to create towel holders, or better yet, shelves, which will do double duty as storage or display. A small bathroom that is very beautiful is often nicer than a large bathroom. I put a lot of time and energy into decorating our very small bathroom; many have commented on its beauty and size, when in reality it is quite tiny.

If necessary, get a bathroom shelf for other storage items. Put in hooks and shelves to handle high traffic and utility. If you have space, a hamper is excellent in the bathroom. Remember to get your family to do regular quick bathroom cleanups. Commercial bathroom wipes also can be used daily by family members to keep the bathroom clean.

Basements

Basements are notorious for being glorified storage rooms. Do not accumulate things Store items in boxes. Mark each box. Purge using the quadrant method. You do this by dividing the basement into four parts and determining the purpose of each quadrant. This is the same as when you determined the purpose of each room.

When in doubt, throw it out. Get shelving to accommodate hobbies and needed storage. Do not just put it there and forget it. If you do not use it seasonally, then why are you storing it? If it is a memento, then when do you plan to regularly reminisce? Think about getting heavy-duty storage units or shelving for basement storage.

Label all storage. Instead of just placing boxes in the basement, assign numbers to the boxes. Write down their contents on index cards, so that you can quickly retrieve anything from those boxes without a lot of effort.

Garage

Don't just put it there and forget it. This area can likewise be made more purposeful simply by dividing it into quadrants and determining the purpose of each quadrant. Store like items together. Put as many things on the walls as possible. Bicycle racks are rather commonplace now, as are tool holders. You can even draw an outline of your car in the middle of the garage, so that you can organize everything around your car fitting into the garage. For safety's sake, absolutely everything in your garage should be labeled. You can also get a shed or be creative with other outdoor storage. An all-weather patio bench might have storage space in its seat.

Office

Do not mix your personal documents with your business items. Purge your papers and do not pile them. You should clean your desk daily. Even if you are working on a project, your desk should be clean. Place work in an active folder, but never leave work all over your desk. A cluttered desk makes for a cluttered mind. File office papers regularly. Make certain everything on your desk is well within reach. You can store small items like pencils and pens in a larger storage unit. It can be frustrating to look for small items. Capitalize on your computer for keeping track of materials.

There is a lot of organizing software and economical office material available.

Books

Books should be placed on a bookshelf. I know this sounds rather obvious, but I have been in homes where the books have overtaken the family living space. Quite frankly, at times, our family's books have been all over, as if they were breeding faster than rabbits in heat. To keep a handle on your book situation, limit the number of books you take into your home. Throw away or donate excess books to libraries, schools, and other organizations. You should throw away outdated books and books in poor condition. Sentimental as you may be about them, they are probably of little value to anyone other than you.

Organize your books by subject and color-code them accordingly. You will find that you tend to read in categories. Typically, my books fall in the following categories: education, children, marriage, business, organization, novels, training, prayer, spiritual growth, finances, health, women, and writing. I use colored stickers that correspond to the different categories I read, so I can easily locate them on the bookshelf. I purchase the small multicolored stickers from an office-supply store. Actually, I am undertaking a major project to use the Library of Congress classification system to label our books. You might not be in this desperate situation, but as a home educator with children of varying ages and grade levels, I need to retrieve books quickly.

Shoes

First, simplify your wardrobe. If you are a shoe enthusiast, there are many shoe-organization devices on the market today, including closet hanging bags and racks. Whichever one you choose, make sure that it has the capacity to hold all your footwear easily.

Linen closet

You should fold the sheet sets together and put the pillowcases inside as well, so you do not have to waste time looking for the matching pillowcases. In addition to folding the sheet sets together, you should also put all full-sized sheet sets together, all twin-sized sets, and so on, as this will alleviate a lot of confusion and wasted time.

Cards

You probably have more birthday and holiday cards then you will ever have the chance to look at again. However, if you are hopelessly sentimental, save cards in a separate box. Put time in your schedule to reread cards. Personally, I save very few cards. I store those I do save in a file-sized box in the basement, where I plan regular times of reminiscing. A lot of people store old cards they will never look at again. This just creates more clutter.

Children's work

I know you just love Junior's animal picture, but to avoid clutter, save only one or two pieces per age or school grade. I know this is hard, but you will appreciate it more when it is neat, organized, and dated (write the date on the back of project), rather than just a mass of papers.

Papers

These should be in the reminiscing box, and please remember that if you do not make regular times of reminiscing, then it is a waste of space in your home. Save one or two papers. Your entire college career should be in a box. Notes should be in your household filing system if they are relevant. If not, they should be tossed.

Magazines, sales circulars, and advertisements

Each time a new magazine comes into your house, toss the old issue. Leave old magazines in the dentist's office, at the pediatrician's, etc. There should be a place in your home for these. Immediately throw out the ones you do not regularly shop in, and of course, throw out the old ones before you take in the new. Handle every piece of paper in your home once.

Kids

Many of our children have an overabundance of stuff. Children's rooms should have zones, or specific areas of purpose. Encourage your child to divide his or her room into quadrants. You may then assign a purpose to each portion of the room. Typical zones could be toy, game, doll, racing-car, and reading zones. Rotate toys so that your child has ample time to miss certain toys and to keep their stuff organized.

A place for everything

Finally, you need a place for everything, and everything should be in its place. Everything absolutely needs a place. Everything needs a specific place, or else chaos will reign. If you look back at the house-plan assignment, you will recognize that in order to have order, everything must be in its proper place. When you are having difficulty maintaining order, it generally stems from one of these areas:

Indecision: You have not settled on a permanent place for the item(s), or it is a relatively new place, and a positive habit needs to be established.

No focus: You have items scattered all over the place. Examples of this are the junk drawer and the closet with everything in it, including the bowling balls. Every item in your home needs to be categorized or assigned its own space.

Undue sentiment: You have items that need to be thrown away, yet you have not done so.

Habit not formed: You are still working on forming a new habit. It generally takes about twenty-one days to form a new habit. To be efficient, make decisions quickly, reward yourself for new habits, and simplify your home regularly. Every time any item arrives in your home, throw away or give away a similar item. This is especially true of clothing. When purchasing a new blouse, throw away or give away an article of clothing before placing the new blouse in your closet.

People will cooperate when they know what is expected of them. Children should be given weekly chore charts. These charts should be posted where everyone can see them. The chores should be appropriate to the child's emotional and physical capabilities. Family members should also be rewarded for completing tasks.

Prayer

Lord Jesus, guide me in this special calling to make my home a place where your presence dwells, a safe haven where your word is daily reflected in our activities. May my life and home nourish my family physically, emotionally, and spiritually. May your word be a lamp to my feet and a light to my path as I order my life according to your purposes for my life and my family. In Jesus's name, amen.

Quick Tips

- Do two or more things at the same time. For instance, clear off your desk while speaking on the telephone.
- Get up early. Studies show that working one half-hour in the morning is equivalent to staying up three hours at night.
- Guard your personal development and planning time. Put it in your calendar as you would any other important meeting.
- Do not let indecision paralyze you. Keep moving!
- Remove the word "try" from your vocabulary. "Try" implies failure and doubt.
- Disharmony consumes time and energy. Work on your relationships.

- Organize your personal places (home) and professional places (desk). A cluttered desk means a cluttered mind.
- Deal with procrastination. Break large tasks into smaller tasks.
- Follow your instincts. Do not be bullied out of doing what you know is the right thing to do.
- Always evaluate and be ready to make appropriate changes. Cut down on the number of meetings you are attending.
- Eat healthy. Most sickness is diet-related.
- Do something while waiting in line. Read a book. Make a list. Write a card.
- Use your traveling time to listen to a teaching or self-improvement tape.
- Get a cookbook and try different economical recipes.
- Turn off the television immediately once you have reached the allotted time you have decided to watch television.
- Invest in yourself. Take a speed-reading class.
- Use upbeat music to make cleaning your home quicker and fun!
- Mark your car antenna with a bright ribbon so you can quickly locate it in a mall parking lot.
- Make a list of aisles in the supermarket where you usually shop. Write your list according to the aisles.
- Look at a cookbook and make different meals for the week. Do all your shopping for the ingredients at one time.
- Sit down with the family and get help planning and preparing meals.
- Go to the supermarket during off-peak hours (like 6:00 AM). The shelves are usually stocked, and there are no lines.
- Minimize morning chaos by creating a routine. Write it down, so all can agree to it.
- Encourage children to move faster in the morning by offering stickers, incentive-chart rewards, and special breakfasts.
- Make pancakes the night before and put them in the refrig-

erator for all to enjoy.
- Buy items in bulk.
- Use a timer in the morning to time your routine, then try to break your own record.
- Use television times to do ironing or fold laundry.
- Buy via mail order when possible. Avoid lines.
- Invest in a cordless telephone, and call a friend while you do household chores like cooking or cleaning.
- Keep magnets handy in your home office to pick up staples, paper clips, etc.
- Set out all your clothes, including all accessories, the night before.
- Always put two sets of clothing out for babies and young children.
- Hang all your clothes and accessories for the day on one hanger.
- Buy trial-sized items, so you are prepared for unexpected trips.
- When packing, pack light, so you can carry your bag on the airplane.
- When cooking, take a spoon or a spatula with you into another room to remind you that food is cooking.

Chapter 11

A MOTHER'S CALLING

The things we see—order, cleanliness, and cooperation—were made by the things we do not see, such as love, peace, joy, and patience.

Ultimately, the spiritual atmosphere in your home governs its physical atmosphere. Christian homes can be very legalistic, ruled by law, and enforced by anger and punishment—or your home can be ordered by love and enforced by the spirit of God. You can set the atmosphere of your home. The decision is up to you.

Mothers are special. I am blessed to have two mothering examples in my life. My mother and my mother-in-the-Lord (as I refer to her, because the term mother-in-law has negative connotations) are two dynamic ladies. My mother (along with my father) managed to raise seven children who did not become statistics. I am indebted to my mother-in-the-Lord for perhaps her greatest achievement—the way she influenced my husband (although both of his parents contributed significantly). In addition, God has provided me with a plethora of others with mothers' hearts in the church community. Surely, mothers are a precious part of the body of Christ.

As moms, the way we juggle our time can be quite a feat. Time is different when you are a mom. Your schedule is primarily dictated by the needs of others. I once heard someone say that Jesus really understood mothers. During his entire earthly ministry, He rarely had a moment to himself. He was followed everywhere he went by twelve guys who often just could not get the point. He did not get discouraged, even though he spent three years pouring into their lives. He just kept his eye on the prize: the salvation of their souls. As mothers, we need this same eternal perspective.

We need to embrace our mothering challenges, understanding the eternal implications. It is easy to fall into the mundane day-to-day activities and to lose our eternal perspective among the dirty diapers. It is important that we remind ourselves of the following principles.

Children are a gift from the Lord.

They are not our burdens to bear, but rather our crowns to wear. Children are not excess packages that weigh you down or keep you from reaching your personal goals, yet often this is the way children are treated in church. I often see parents active in ministry whose children flounder because no accommodations are made for them. When God called men and women to ministry, he called whole families. Christ gets no glory when you sacrifice your children's destiny on the altar of church service.

Involve your children in your ministry. In fact, God's perfect plan for evangelism is that parents birth their children into the kingdom, then disciple them accordingly. It is not the Sunday-school teacher's responsibility to teach your child the word, it is yours! Raise your child up in the reverential fear and admonition of the Lord. Teach them while they are young. Give them your time unselfishly. Love them, and they will grow to love your God as well. Unfortunately, the converse is also true. Too many church children turn away from God because of the hurt, neglect, and rejection they felt as church children. Do not provoke your children to wrath. Be their mom first. Love them with your time and attention, and they will grow to love God.

Progress and activity are not synonymous.

Besides limiting your activities, your child needs restrictions on her activities. Some kids are involved in so many things that their home is nothing more than a hotel and their parents are glorified chauffeurs. I strongly believe many children are involved in so many activities due to parental guilt and fear. Parents fear their children not being competitive enough. Others lack the backbone to say no to their children's unreasonable requests. They fall prey to the way the world raises their children. Christian moms should determine their children's schedule after consultation with the Lord. Too often, decisions are reached for the wrong reasons.

This is illustrated in the fervor with which we indiscriminately place our children in different activities. Once a mom called me while a television show featuring various child prodigies was airing; a toddler on the show was playing a magnificent piano symphony. Watching it, she excitedly panted, "I must get piano lessons for my child."

Knowing her child had neither musical aptitude nor inclination, I asked why.

"Because," she impatiently whined, "I want him to play like that. We have to do it so our kids can keep up with all the others," she said, trying to draw me into her irrational reasoning.

Our children's activities should be based on their individual gifts and their callings. And moms, you can only know their gifts and callings as a result of prayer and communion with the Holy Spirit. Remember, the scripture tells us that after observing events in young Jesus's life, "Mary held these things in her heart." We know that she was a prayerful woman to be entrusted with the savior of the world. She knew how to listen to the Holy Spirit. We too can do this with our children.

Sometimes the Holy Spirit may lead us to expose our children to different activities for a season, yet these activities should never interfere with family life or your child's spiritual development. Remember, your child needs time to be a child too. A hectic schedule can also cause a child premature stress. The most important progress your child can make is spiritual progress. No activity can replace the presence of God.

An empty vessel has nothing to pour.

You need time alone with God. This is not optional. You *need* time to fill yourself so that you can pour into others. Mothers are constantly pouring. Your children are the major benefactors of your time alone with God. My children do not interrupt me when I am praying. (Of course, I trained them not to.) But they know I am more patient, kind, and long-suffering after I have been in the presence of God. Since you are responsible for your children's spiritual development, you should be reading, studying, and praying, so that they can receive the overflow of your time with God. Most mothers do not spend time alone with God, so they have little to give, or they try to give with their own strength. Moms should minister to their children in the power of the Holy Spirit.

One of my spiritual mentors, the late Susanna Wesley (mother of the godly Wesley brothers), home-schooled her brood of nineteen and left a lasting legacy for us all. She was a fantastic preacher who brought forth the word boldly in public as well as in her home. She sparked a great revival in her town. She was known to put her apron over her head and pray right in the midst of her noisy household. She knew when she was in danger of doing things with her own strength as opposed to God's strength. She left a fantastic legacy for us as mothers.

You are not your role.

A few dear friends refer to me as "Mama Carter." Interestingly, this has never bothered me, because they realize that I look after them spiritually, keeping them in prayer and occasionally challenging their spiritual position. I am proud of that title. Still, I find that many moms do not have identities of their own; their children are their lives. Being absorbed in children results in mothers circumventing even the very things God may be calling them to do. In other words, their lives are their children. Everyone needs to develop his or her own interests, gifts, and talents. A mom is not the sum total of all we are to God.

I was a wife before I was a mother. Many women fail to realize this. Mothers also need to develop their relationship with their husbands. My husband and I still date, although we have been married fourteen years. Yes, we actually date—without the kids. It keeps our romance alive and definitely revitalizes me.

Mothering is a seasonal commitment.

I am often reminded, usually by an elderly couple strolling in the park, to appreciate my children while they are young. These seniors often say this with a look of regret, sadness in their voices, and a forlorn look in their eyes. I do not want to be like these people.

One day, I will release my children to go out into the world to fully live out their callings. They will, one day, walk and talk with God alone in the cool of the day. There will be no more runny noses to wipe, no more dirty laundry to clean, no more "because I said so, that's why," and no more sleepless nights. On that day, my husband and I will stroll in the park, and upon seeing a young couple, we will say, with a twinkling gleam in our eyes and joy in our voices, "Enjoy them now." We will do this knowing that we did enjoy our children, and eagerly awaiting the inheritance of our grandchildren!

May the Lord continue to gently lead you as you guide your

children. May the joys of motherhood outweigh your regrets!

Quick Tips

- Be flexible. Being rigid produces stress.
- Learn to say no without guilt.
- Take your infant or toddler in the shower with you. Use suction baby bath ring.
- Get rid of outdated clothes you have not worn in over a year.
- Mark your luggage with brightly colored ribbons, so you can locate your luggage at the airport quickly.
- Write and recite a daily biblical confession that will empower you as a mom.
- Plan a "mom's night out" with other mothers.
- Smile more often!
- Join with other mothers to help you achieve your personal goals. You may even form a personal improvement club.
- Listen to book on tapes. Join an audio book club.

Chapter 12

FREQUENTLY ASKED TIME-MANAGEMENT QUESTIONS

Time is a gift.

You mentioned the two kinds of daily planning or scheduling. In one method, you list your roles or goals, then the activities that relate to them. In the other, you list everything you have to do, and approach the tasks from most important to least important. Which one do you prefer? Why?

Generally, I prefer to list my roles or goals and the corresponding tasks under each heading. Because I am more concerned about the quality of my life than the quantity of my days, my choices are made around my convictions. I do so many different things, and this method keeps me centered. If I do a lot of counseling and neglect my family, I can verify it in one day, because it is right before me in black and white. Generally, I will seek the Lord's guidance about which roles he desires me to plan for daily. I do prefer the numerical method when I have a lot to do or when I am feeling slightly overwhelmed, because that method gets it all out on paper and I can determine what I want to do first. It all depends on the individual. There are no right or wrong methods here.

How do you do it all?

I do not do it all. I once heard someone say, "Balance precludes all my roles or goals being equal." They simply are not. Balance occurs over the long haul of life. I may put more time into mothering with my children while they are quite young than I will when they are older. I may work a little less on my business at some times more than others. It is a matter of prioritizing. I realize I cannot do it all, and I just do what is most important to me. I stay close to God, so I don't get off track. That's where knowing your values comes into place. If you know your values, you will not be pushed into doing something that will stress you and make you unproductive.

In the workshop, you said that procrastination is inner conflict. How can this be? I know I really want to go back to school and get my degree, but things I can't control keep coming up. I cannot think of any reasons not to do it, but I keep putting getting my degree off.

Well, you first need to ask yourself why you want a degree, then probe very deeply into why you do not want one. The excuses you give for not doing it might reveal the real issue, especially if you have procrastinated for so long. There is a law of human behavior that states that we move toward the pleasurable. It may be that you are running from something that requires work. On the other hand, you may be procrastinating because you do not have a clear goal in mind. Why do you want to go to school? What are the benefits? What might be the liabilities for you, personally, if you went to school now? There is still another issue here. Is this your own goal, or are you doing it because someone says you should go to school? In this case, you may be rebelling against authority unconsciously. Or are you waiting for everything to be perfect in your personal life before you go to school? This type of procrastination is rooted in perfectionism. Things will never be to your complete satisfaction. Also, the fact that you say things you cannot control keep coming up reveals, to a degree, that you are not really settled on going back to school. Probe yourself; you have all the answers.

How can I get more out of my time?

The only way to get more out of your time is to pour more into yourself. Take a speed-reading course or a continuing education course, read good books, and make certain you have quiet time every day. You should also exercise regularly and eat well, as both give you energy and stamina. It may seem simplistic, but it really works!

Can you recommend a good planner or organizer?

I do not prefer one type to another. I can tell you the features to look for in a good one. You should be able to see a month at a glance. It should also have adequate space on the daily planning pages to jot down notes. It should be attractive, and small enough for you to carry with you almost everywhere. Most women prefer theirs to fit in their purses. I like a fairly large planner, because I use it for both home and business. I need large spaces to write on. Some planners are needlessly expensive. Visit a large office-supply store and check out their available stock. Franklin Covey is a very popular planner/organizer. Electronic organizers are also becoming more popular.

My kids take up all my free time. They need me. What can I do?

Children need to be taught responsibility. (I will assume you are giving them more than adequate attention.) The next step is to train your kids to be more responsible for themselves. You really are not doing a service to your children when you do everything for them. They should be gradually growing more responsible for things in the home and for their own choices. I once spoke with a mother who was very tired because she had been to her daughter's school three times that week because the child left homework on the table. The child, in effect, had no responsibility and continued to demand more of her mother. The mother thought all children were irresponsible, and she never allowed the daughter to suffer the consequences of forgetting her homework. Be careful, and give your children room to grow.

Can you further explain values?
Values are what are most important to you. All of us have values. The priority we place on values helps us to determine our goals. Values are the internal motivators each of us possesses. All of our activities are the result of our values. If we love the Lord, then he should motivate us. Our values should mirror our relationship with him, for it is he who gives us our passions and goals. Of course, even Christians have different passions; for instance, one may feel a strong call to missions, while another may feel passionate about ministering to children. Their passions will determine how they spend their time and money. If you really want to know what is important to you, look at the way you spend your money and your time.

I have so much to do. How can I have a meaningful moment every day?
Great question. A meaningful moment is just that—a moment. It does not take long. Most times, we think of little thoughtful things we want to do all the time. However, we never seem to get to do it. A meaningful moment ensures that we send a card, make a call, smile, and say thank you. It takes so little time; it can almost seem insignificant.

Do you have any suggestions for working mothers?

Yes. You should definitely be scheduling meaningful moments with your children every day. Remember, little things like "I love you" do matter. Work hard, so that presents do not become a substitute for your presence. Be certain to have a quiet time, so you can have more to give out. Create morning and evening routines for your kids. Try not to bring the job home with you. I know that's a lot. Also remember to cultivate a relationship with your husband. Schedule family time regularly, and be careful not to over-commit.

You spoke about setting a goal for quiet time. I am still trying to have quiet time. Isn't that my goal?

No, not really. A goal draws you to it. If you want to have quiet time because I (or anyone else) said you should, this is not a goal. In fact, most likely, it will cause you to procrastinate. You need to decide for yourself why you want to have a quiet time daily. Do you want to know the Lord more personally? Only quiet time can cultivate a relationship with the Lord.

How do I develop good habits?

Good habits are developed by discipline. It will take time. Generally, it takes twenty-one days to establish a habit. Force yourself to be consistent for this time span. Reward yourself for each step of progress you make. It will be uncomfortable at first, but the benefits are great.

Are the words I speak to myself really that important?

Yes, because your words express your thinking. You will always move in the direction of your most dominant thoughts.

You keep stressing a woman having time alone. Why? It doesn't bother me that I have very little time alone.

A recent survey asked women what they wanted more of.

Time was the number one response. This is not surprising. Studies show that women have a real need to have time alone. Granted, some personalities require very little time alone. Still, the vast majority of women need time alone; that is why I stress quiet time so much. Most women tell me that they wish they had more time. Some read a book, listen to music, or even dance when they are by themselves. Others take long, hot baths or play a game of solitaire. As you enjoy being with yourself, so will others enjoy being with you.

How does a mother with four children all under the age of nine get any quiet time?

This is a question very dear to my heart. Susanna Wesley, the mother of John and Charles Wesley, major founders of the Methodist denomination, had nineteen children. She was known to pull her apron over her head and pray. Her kids learned not to disturb Mom when the apron was over her head, and I surmise that she knew how to tune out the noise. I find that sometimes I have to quiet myself internally and pray in small snatches of time. This is not always the best way, but I have found that it works for me. My children also know not to disturb me when I go into my bedroom and close the door. Also, when I used to get up with the babies at night, I used it as an opportunity to pray for the child and to have a little prayer time myself. Because I home-school, my children are with me nearly all the time, and I have learned to commune with God right in the midst of the chaos. It is not easy, but I have to get my quiet time in. Try to get time in the morning, even for brief periods, or pray during their naptime. You can also train your children to play by themselves or read to give you a bit of quiet time.

I feel so guilty when I say no to people. I know I need to say no more often. What do you recommend?

Most girls were raised to be people pleasers. Couple this with our desire to be liked and accepted, and I can understand your dilemma. You need to listen to the words you say to yourself and make your own goals. This will make it easier to say no without guilt. Incidentally, I do not believe we should say no to everything, but I do feel that many women are over-committed in many of their activities.

I give my kids quality time, yet they still demand a lot of me. What can I do? I want some "me time."
Quality time is a myth. Quality time is born of quantity time. The more time I spend with those I love, the more quality I put in the relationship. I also suggest that you concentrate on being in a good mood and with a listening ear more often, because kids know when you are truly there for them. In addition, if you are forced, through circumstances beyond your control, to spend very little time with your kids, then I urge you to reexamine your schedule and to put your kids in your schedule before they have to ask you for some time. You may need to organize yourself a bit more and see where you can take time from other things. Be honest with yourself.

My husband doesn't respect my time. He is always giving me things to do and infringing on my time. What can I do?
Begin by sharing your goals with your husband. It is a good practice to get a planner and have a meeting with him to equitably discuss one another's goals and plans. Most times, I find wives are reluctant to make their own goals and to establish plans with their mates. Prayerfully consider having a weekly family-planning session to share with one another.

I am a working mother. The mornings are really crazy. What should I do?
You need a schedule in the morning that everyone can agree on. Write out how you would like your morning to flow. Identify

the trouble spots. Do as much preparation the night before as you can. Limit kids' clothing choices. Make sure kids get enough sleep the night before. Use a timer—let kids try to beat the clock brushing their teeth, getting dressed, etc. Make a special breakfast. We usually have pancakes on Saturday. I usually make extra. I freeze them and offer them as an incentive breakfast on mornings when we have to be out the house early. There are very good commercial frozen foods you might try. The kids put stickers by each item on a chart after they complete a task. Tasks can be simple, like brushing their teeth or making their beds. For some reason, the kids love accumulating sticker sheets.

Chapter 13

FREQUENTLY ASKED HOME-MANAGEMENT QUESTIONS

Clear goals are like magnets. They draw us to greatness

Your ideas sound good, but it seems everything is rush, rush, and rush. I want to slow down.

You are right. I really want people to slow down. Once you write your mission statement, perhaps a strong characteristic of your home might be a less hectic pace. Reduce your outside activities; schedule quality time with your husband and kids. You can set the tone of your home.

Help, I'm always running out of groceries! Any suggestions?

Post a list on the refrigerator, and when you get low on an item put it on the list. (The list should also correspond to the aisles of the supermarket you shop at most.) Also, plan menus so you can get all shopping done at one time. Go through a good cookbook and make a master list of menus you can use. You can even use different themes for each day. For instance, you can eat Italian on Mondays; therefore, you need four different Italian dishes for each Monday in the month. Tuesday could be vegetarian day. Of course, Saturday could be kids' menus. It really works.

No matter what I do, I forget something by the time I pack up my four kids and put them in the van. What am I doing wrong?
Nothing. I commend you! With four kids, it is nearly impossible to remember everything. I suggest that you have a diaper bag that always stays packed. When you come into the house after a trip, immediately replace any diapers or clothes used. Let the kids have their own travel bags with extra clothes, juice, snacks, and caps. This should help you have less on your mind. I hope that helps. In my family, the kids also have bags with some of their toys, because sometimes my speaking engagements go into overtime. Here again is where the concept of checklists is essential.

I know it is a little thing, but it really annoys me when my daughter uses my comb and I have to search for it.
You are not alone. Small items are hard to keep up with. Try using a small basket. Take the whole basket with you when you are using an item. It is easier to search for a basket than a hair comb. I use them for nail clippers, tweezers, etc. It really helps.

Everything is a mess—where do I start?
Begin with what annoys you the most. Work at a little bit day by day. Determine what is causing the disorder, and start there. Do not try to achieve absolute order in one day; you'll only get discouraged.

Help, I'm cleaning all the time!

Examine your standard of cleanliness: is it too high? Are you training others in your household to help? Are your expectations unreasonable because you have small children? Also, look at the things you are constantly cleaning. Adapt to instinctive human habits. For instance, if kids are throwing their coats on the living room floor, perhaps you can provide eye-level hooks for them. Or if your husband is prone to leave his muddy work boots in the foyer, perhaps you can put a mat in the foyer to accommodate the boots. If you are cleaning all the time, you are serving your house; it is not serving you.

My husband is so messy. I just can't take it at times. What should I do?

What habits of his can you accommodate and which ones can you eliminate? You can put a box at the door for his shoes, or use a quilt holder or chair in the living room to place clothes on instead of the bedroom floor. Besides this, you might try talking with him. Show him your mission statement; get his input. Approach the subject when you are not upset. Enlist his help in running the home. Make it more of a partnership. Be willing to listen if your standards are too high.

I'm a home-schooling mother, and it seems that my housework is never done. What can I do?

Wow, what a great opportunity to involve your kids in real-life skills! Integrate your teaching time with cleaning. Assign chores to everyone, and make sure the chores are done before schoolwork. In addition, you can make cooking and common household chores actual schoolwork. Occasionally, when things get really chaotic in my home, we have a family cleaning day. Besides cleaning, we use it as a time to talk with one another. The children can also help figure out why some places are prone to being more messy than others. In this way, they are motivated to keep the house in order. Of course, you should teach your children the purpose principle. Home-schooling offers such a great opportunity to teach home management to our sons and daughters. Remember also to teach your children to do the work, rather than doing it for them. Little ones can learn sorting by doing the laundry. Use incentive charts and stickers to motivate kids. Relax your standard of cleanliness, because as a home educator, the rooms in your home probably have a multitude of purposes. Strive to be effective, not neat as a pin. Phyllis Diller once said, "Cleaning your house when you have small children is like shoveling while it is still snowing." Enjoy your kids. Enjoy your home.

I'm a stay-at-home mother whose home is out of control. Help, please!

When your family is home all day, your home naturally has a tendency to become disorderly more frequently. Enjoy your home. Strive for effectiveness, not perfection. Try involving the kids in the cleaning and organizing process. Remember also that you are serving your family, not your house.

My kids undo everything I do almost immediately. What should I do?

House rules will help in this area for older children. They should be restricted in some areas until they prove they can be responsible. You may need to slightly change your decor when you have toddlers or preschoolers who can get into everything. Try putting things out of reach. Have a section where they can play with toys. There should be some consequence for them making things disorderly so quickly; likewise, you should reward them for helping you to keep the house clean and tidy. This is a hard one even for me.

I want my house to be clean and neat all the time. Is that asking too much of my family?

Well, it might be. Although I have not spoken much about it, you should be aware of the atmosphere of your home. Love or law can rule a home. Law says you obey every rule in this house—no exceptions, no mercy. The house becomes more important than the relationships in the house. This kind of home will be spotlessly clean, but it will radiate a kind of shallowness. A person like this serves her home. Or your home can be ruled by love. Shoes should not be in the living room, but if your son comes home and throws them there after his team was defeated in the playoffs, what should you do? Pick up the shoes, encourage your son, and offer to make him his favorite meal. See the difference? It is my prayer that people attending my workshops will design homes ruled by love, not law.

I live in a studio. How can I apply the purpose and activities exercise?

You can divide the studio into four quadrants. Picture invisible walls, and determine the purpose of each section. This also works for a large room or a small room if you have limited space.

I do not like house cleaning. I spend too much time doing it. Any suggestions?

I spend very little time cleaning. I do "o'clock" the rooms almost daily, though. Once the rooms are cleaned, you can "o'clock" them at the end of the day—particularly when the kids go to bed. You can train your older children to "o'clock" their bedrooms and playrooms. Basically, you can reduce cleaning by organizing, then daily maintenance, and by not dedicating so much time to cleaning just for beauty. Purchase the right cleaning products and give the chemicals time to work before you wipe counters, etc. Also, use a timer and try to clean rooms more quickly. Make a game out of it, and it will be fun.

I have a newborn, and my house is really out of order. What can I do?

Rest and enjoy your newborn. Relax your standards a bit. This is just a season. Your baby will grow up so fast.

My boys share a room. One is very messy and the other is neat. Their bickering usually centers on how the room is kept. What can I do?

It may be necessary to literally draw an invisible line down the middle of the room. Or you can make a list of acceptable standards they both agree on, perhaps also teaching the messy one to "o'clock" his room. This can be an excellent learning experience for when they go away to college.

I'm a single mother in school, working full time, and I don't have time for much of anything. It seems that every day I am exhausted, and then I start the same procedure the next day. I know I'm doing what I supposed to be doing, but it is all so hard. Is there any way I can organize my home in one evening?

No, unfortunately there is not, but the time you invest in organizing your home, even if it is just in small steps, can radically change your life and that of your children. I also suggest that you read my book, "Organize Your Life," to help you work on your daily scheduling skills and reaching your goals. Goals should energize us. Yes, they are hard work, but it sounds like you may be doing things just because someone else said you should do it.

I have eight kids, and the work seems endless. Help!

Someone once told me that housework is like painting the Golden Gate Bridge. This bridge is painted year-round, because when they begin painting one side of the bridge, the other needs painting. Housework is an ongoing process. When your children are all gone, your house will be neat as a pin. Of course, the grandchildren are not far behind at that point. In the meantime, try training them to do household tasks, and relax your standards. It may help to have one room that is neat all the time. I used to do this with our living room. I could open the door on a clean, clutter-free room when my kids were toddlers.

Even after I have determined the purpose of each room in my house, I still keep getting messes in my kitchen. What can I do?

There are a few possibilities here. One is that you must narrow the focus of your purpose. Is there a lot happening in your kitchen? Perhaps you were too vague or broad in determining the purpose of your kitchen. Another possibility is that there are many purposes for that one room, and naturally, that room gets the most clutter. If the other rooms in your home are relatively clutter-free, then don't worry about it. However, you should first look at why the messes are occurring. Might you need to reorganize your kitchen?

Can you share how you balance all the different things you do?

Yes. I just don't do it all. I think Bob Yandian said it best: "I do not balance all my roles." Balance suggests that each role is equally important. That is simply not the case. My role as mother may supersede my role as organizer. Of course, when my children are grown, my mothering role should decrease in importance, and therefore take less time. Think of balance over the totality of your life, not just in a moment of time. Sometimes we only see where we are right now. That is why it is important to set goals. Decide what is important, and do it. When doing housework, try to do two things at once. Typically, I fold the laundry while listening to a teaching tape or watching a favorite television broadcast. I even invite the kids to help by getting them involved in a conversation. I do this with cooking too. Sometimes there are more opportunities to talk with our family members than we realize. Often my husband will come into the kitchen and write and discuss the bills while I am cooking. So when thinking about doing two things at once, think of ways you can build your relationships. I try to do as many things with my children as I do for them. This keeps our home and our relationships great.

My husband is neater than I am, and it is driving me batty. What can I do?

You probably won't get a lot of sympathy on this question, but I understand you. It can be a real blow to a woman's self-esteem when her mate is a better housekeeper than she is. I suggest open communication. Primarily, you can just work with him to develop a way to communicate his expectations without being critical. It is the same as if the situation were reversed: decide that your relationship is more important than the house.

How do I keep my kids out my home office?

You don't. Give them some toys. You can even keep special toys they can only play with when you are on a business call. Try to involve them in your home-office procedures as much as possible. That way, when you need to work, they have an understanding of what you are doing. My son checks my e-mail for me, so he knows when I am going to be pretty busy. Parents who work and have infants: I strongly suggest their crib or playpen not be placed in the office. There should be a door or something that can serve as a sound barrier if you need to take a telephone call. Also, when all else fails, use the mute button on your telephone. You can still hear your customer, and it gives you time to calm a crying baby or to quiet fussy children. Use the family calendar, too, to post any projects you are currently working on. Your files should be separate from your home files. Get on our mailing list; we are developing a workshop called "Running an Efficient Home Office."

Can you suggest a simple meal-management plan?

You can get a calendar and plan different themes for each day of the week. For instance, on Mondays you could serve vegetarian meals. Tuesdays you could serve Italian meals. Wednesdays you could serve Mexican, Thursdays could be kids' meals. Each day of the week can have a special theme. Then figure out five meals in each of those themes. You choose five meals because inevitably, some months will have a fifth weekday in them. Then you simply rotate the meals monthly. You can also have a fall/winter menu as well as a spring/summer menu plan. Once you have made a master menu, then you can make a master shopping list. It takes a bit of time to initiate, but it pays off in the long run.

Chapter 14

FREQUENTLY ASKED QUESTIONS ABOUT ORGANIZING CHILDREN AND TEENAGERS

Time does not heal old wounds. It gives us the space to change our reaction to the hurt.

I have a daughter who is really neat, and another who is incredibly sloppy. They are constantly at each other's throats, especially when it's time to clean up their room. What can I do?

Talk to them both about compromising on a standard of cleanliness. Let them both agree on an acceptable standard. This can be done by actually writing down what each of them considers "clean." Children who are more creative sometimes have a bit of difficulty understanding that their environment is not orderly. They just need someone to lovingly point it out to them. Also, teach them to "o' clock" their room at the end of the day. You "o'clock" a room by starting at the position of twelve o' clock, then moving clockwise, cleaning everything in the specified area until you return to twelve o'clock. This way, a child does not get overwhelmed, but has a way to approach disorder. Both of them can learn a lot about compromise and positive problem-solving if you work with them.

My two-year-old will undo everything I have done in a minute. I feel like I won't have an orderly home until he's twenty-one. What can I do?

There are few things you can do besides praying that he grows up quickly. Make specific play areas for him. Give him some chores he can do, like dusting. It will help if he thinks it is also his responsibility to keep things in order. Two-year-olds really like to do what they see others doing. They will imitate whatever you emphasize for them.. Capitalize on this trait and let him help keep the house in order. It's worth a try. Also, begin to train your two-year-old to clean up after himself. Use a cleanup-time song.

My ten-year-old gives me such a hassle about doing homework. She wastes so much time looking for little things. What can I do?

Make sure she has a quiet place to do her homework. Also, make sure you have a homework box with the necessary crayons, pens, pencils, paper, and other materials.

With five kids, whenever we have to go anywhere as a family, it's a major production! I'm starting to feel like I don't ever want to leave my house. Any suggestions?

Before you resign yourself to a life as a hermit—although, with five kids, it is certainly understandable—enlist the help of all the kids. Give each child a task to do each time you go out. Make up a list of everything that generally has to be done: packing diaper bags, snacks, and changes of clothes; closing the windows; etc. Also, give yourself at least twenty more minutes than you think you will need to get out the house on time. Reward kids generously for their cooperative behavior. Make it a pleasant experience for your kids. Depending on the ages of your kids, an exit checklist might work well. (An exit checklist simply lists everything that has to be done before you leave the house). Above all, start planning early.

How can I help my children keep their clothes in order?
Put actual pictures on the dresser drawers. For instance, put a picture of a sock on the sock drawer. Older children just require the words to be written on their dresser drawers. You can also purchase drawer dividers. Use different-colored laundry baskets so your children can put away their own clothes. Also, make sure hampers are in the areas where your kids take off their clothes.

I have kid's books and toys all over the house. Help!
Designate areas in your home just for reading and playing. Also, organize kids' books by authors or subjects.

How do you get kids to help out if they ignore the chore chart?
Sometimes they really need some incentive to complete their chores. Perhaps giving them stickers (or some other small reward) will encourage them to perform chores until the chores become a matter of habit.

My kids start crying whenever I throw out their junk. I get very angry. It's just junk: broken toys, old pictures, and silly things like store coupons. What can I do about this?
It is not junk! Imagine how you would feel if someone threw out your prized possessions, just because they didn't seem important. Give the child the opportunity to part with some of his pos-

sessions and to neatly store the remainder. I understand that there will be times when you may slowly get the kids to part with things by getting rid of some things while they are sleeping or just not present. Be sensitive to your children's needs, though. Also, a plastic shoebox is a good place for them to keep their mementos.

My daughter throws her coat on the floor as soon as she comes home. I constantly remind her to hang it up. What can I do?

Make sure she has an eye-level hook to hang her coat on. Also, encourage her to take off her coat in the room where the hook actually is.

My son will often give me a trip note or an important letter for school on the morning of the trip or event. He gets upset if I won't sign it right then. What can I do? Reminders and threats don't seem to work.

Make a folder or an in-box where he puts all of his notes from school in one place every day when he comes home from school. This way, you just have to make sure to check the in-box every evening. You may have to remind him a few times in the beginning.

My kids like to draw and do art projects. Paper, crayons, and all sorts of things are all over the house. Help!

This is an important question. I really do understand, all too well. Make an art box. Put all the art supplies in there. Children should have one designated place to do their art projects. This may work for your little artists, for awhile.

Can you recommend a good toy box?

As a rule, I dislike toy boxes. Toys break in toy boxes, and it is too overwhelming for a young child who just wants to play with one special toy. Shelves and small plastic shoe boxes work best, because they don't frustrate children.

My nine-year-old son has a really bad attitude whenever I try to get him to help out in the house.
Perhaps you need to work on your relationship with your son at the same time you are building his cleaning and organizing skills. Try to make it a fun time, and use it to build your relationship. For instance, you can both make dinner while discussing his school day. You can dust together while you ask him some open-ended questions. (Open-ended questions are not yes-or-no questions, but questions that actually promote conversation. For instance, ask him to describe the perfect teacher.)

Where can I get student planner or organizer?
I prefer the student organizers that college students use, because they have space to integrate the personal and scholastic parts of a young person's life. You can find them at any college bookstore. I have used the Scholastic planners for very young students (www.Scholastic.com). A teen can also use an adult planner if she is really serious about managing her time.

My daughter is so driven—she tells me there is nothing she can cut from her schedule. What can I do?
This can be a positive trait. She probably really needs to put more time into the goal-setting process. She needs to stagger the completion dates of her goals. You do not want to extinguish her zeal, but neither do you want her to burn out or grow up handling too much, which will result in a myriad of health problems.

My child really cannot help herself. She is just six years old. What can I do? I feel so stressed.
You are a classic overworked mom. I once spoke with a friend who was very tired. When I asked why, she really did not seem to know. Later in the conversation, she revealed what was surely the reason for her tiredness. Her schedule had been interrupted

rather abruptly three times in one week. She had been to her child's school three times that week because the child had left school assignments on the kitchen table. When I spoke to her about addressing the child's irresponsibility, she countered by saying that all children are alike, and they simply cannot be taught to be responsible. That is simply not true. All children need to be taught skills that make them more responsible, and therefore more successful, in life. This is best done while the child is young. Please take a child's emotional and physical maturity into account when making guidelines for responsible behavior. Be firm but fair when setting expectations for your child. A child will learn best in the context of a loving relationship with an adult who will take the time to teach skills the child needs to develop. These skills will become good habits that will propel your child into success. A child's life success largely depends on developing good personal habits. A child needs to develop good habits in his personal and academic life. An irresponsible child at home will be one at school as well.

Bedtimes are our family's battle zone. Any suggestions?
Bedtimes need not become a battle zone. Develop a routine. You can use a checklist similar to the one you used to establish a morning routine. Be sure to include a bedtime story, a prayer, or a quiet activity to calm kids down. Be consistent about the bedtime hour. You can even give older siblings a slightly later bedtime. For instance, your seven-year-old might have to be in bed by eight o' clock, whereas your eight-year-old doesn't have to be in bed until 8:15. His fifteen minutes will seem like a big deal to him. It can motivate him to be more responsible in other areas of the home. It can motivate the younger one to be consistent about his bedtime so that he can stay up fifteen minutes later when he is older. It really works. Try it. For infants and toddlers, bedtime can become a real battle zone. Return a toddler to his bed if he keeps getting up. Dr. Sears has a great book on getting your child to sleep: "How

to Get Your Baby to Sleep through the Night."

What about shopping with young children?
This can be a frustrating experience. Avoid it if you can. Trade child care with a friend, or get a teen to watch your kids. If this is not an option, most supermarkets are open twenty-four hours. Go to the store during off-peak hours, like five o'clock in the morning, while the kids are still asleep (Of course, your mate will be at home, watching the children.) If you have no alternative, some supermarkets now have small shopping carts that kids like to push, or you may purchase one for your child. This will actively involve them in the shopping process. Also, prepare children before you get to the supermarket. Tell them what you will purchase and what you will not buy. Reward good behavior with a special treat.

Do you have any ideas on how I can help my child with homework?
Your child should have a relatively quiet spot for homework. His tools for learning should all be there. You can set up a homework box with pencils, pens, a ruler, counting sticks, a protractor, crayons, etc. If your child does her homework at the kitchen table, the box can be bought to the table. You may also want to include coloring books and notebooks for smaller children, who will inevitably want to do "homework" too. Use a kitchen timer for young children, to get them to finish assignments. Play "beat the clock" and have them try to do their math homework in ten minutes. Do this for each subject. Also, review your children's homework with them before they start the assignment. Allow them to read the instructions to you. Ask them to tell you the instructions in their own words. Allow your children to tell you about their day before they begin their homework. They will be able to focus on the task at hand. If children have real difficulty understanding homework, speak to their teachers immediately. Often parents

will not approach a teacher until after an unsatisfactory grade or a poor report card. This is often too late. Use homework to check on your child's school progress.

My children just don't seem to change their habits. What can I do?

Children need motivation to change. Too often, we set goals for our children without their input. Talk to your children. Set goals with them. Find out what they want to achieve, then they will be motivated to achieve. Talk to them about their future. Keep in mind that sometimes children only see the immediate; it can be hard for them to grasp future goals. Make the rewards of their achieving goals as immediate as you can. For instance, while you may need good grades to become a doctor, a child needs a more immediate reward. Reward a good report card with a miniature medical kit, or take the child out on a date. This is more motivating to a child than the reward of becoming a doctor in fifteen years. Tie the reward to the goal. This will encourage your child to set higher goals for himself. You should also give your child the proper tools for success. Every child, beginning in first grade, should have a calendar planner in which to record his assignments. My experiences as an educator have convinced me that most school problems are rarely an issue of comprehension of the material, but rather that the student needs organizing skills. Children should also have proper notebooks. Young children should have three- or five-subject notebooks. Make sure the pages of these notebooks are ruled for primary grades. It is easier to handle one notebook than having separate notebooks for each subject. Older pupils can manage with separate notebooks for each subject. Colored pocket folders are a necessity for school success, no matter what grade the child is in. You can assign a different color for each subject. Young children should have a separate homework folder.

My son constantly forgets his homework books, leaving them at school. We spend so much time calling classmates, trying to get his assignments, that I am just exhausted every evening. What can I do?

To prevent assignments being left at school, post a note with a checklist on your child's homework folder or planner. You can use visual aids, like a picture of a book. The checklist should be very short.

My daughter's desk is so sloppy. What can I do when I can't be with her all the time?

Give her a plastic rectangular pencil case that stays in school. These are available in most office-supply stores. She can use it for her pencils, pens, rulers, crayons, etc. It stays in school. Its purpose is twofold: the child will never be without her supplies in school, and it keeps her desk neat. Explain organizing strategies to her. Teach her that big books go on the bottom and smaller books go on top in her desk. Also, label all textbooks on the spine, especially if the books are covered, which is required in most schools. This sounds very elementary, but sometimes the obvious is not obvious to children.

How can I begin to help my child appreciate time management for school assignments when all he does is play?

Start with his school assignments. Remember that all children should be taught organizational skills early. Have them record assignments in their planners, along with the estimated time to complete the assignment. This is a major time-management skill to master. Even most adults underestimate the actual time it takes to complete a task. As your child practices estimating the time it takes to complete an assignment, he is gaining a valuable skill: the ability to plan.

Remember, planning also involves breaking a task into smaller, more manageable parts. When your child is assigned a book report, help him divide his reading into daily time segments. Encourage him to write these time segments in his planner. Your child will learn accountability. By writing it now, he makes a promise to himself and becomes accountable to you, the parent. He has just conquered procrastination and learned the joy of self-discipline.

How can I teach my child to be a better manager of his time?

A child can learn goal-setting skills easily when he is playing; it is a time when he is highly motivated. Choose something he really wants to learn, such as in-line skating. Break down into small tasks each step that will lead to independent skating, such as "stand in the skates," "walk with the skates," and so on. He will be highly motivated. You can transfer the skills he learns to other areas of his life. Understanding how to set goals and plan can help in school and in his personal life. Reinforce planning skills often. Help your child plan a future family outing. Allow him to figure out what the family will need. These skills learned at leisure will be highly significant, because they will be remembered.

ABOUT THE AUTHOR

Mrs. Carter is the executive director of Organize Your Life! This organization is dedicated to helping individuals and groups reach their maximum productivity and effectiveness. A self-avowed "reformed messy" and a former special-needs teacher, Carter engages her audience with humor, wit, and style. Her personal experiences as an organizing consultant, teacher, trainer, parent, and home educator have meshed perfectly, enabling her to create a dynamic forum in which individuals can realize change in their own lives.

This is evident in the practical application of all her presentations. She gives people real-life solutions, in addition to being motivating and inspiring. She enjoys working with parents, particularly in helping them organize their children and homes and apply time-management principles to their personal lives. It is her heartfelt desire to see mothers love their children in word and deed.

Carter is a clinical member of the National Association of Christian Counselors (NCCA) and is also a prolific author. She has written Christian and secular curricula, as well as parenting and family material. Carter is a columnist for the Long Island, New York *Christian Life Times* and also writes for various online publications. She is the primary home-school teacher for the Carter children (ages eight, eleven, and fourteen) and considers mothering to be her finest achievement.

She is a sought-after speaker on home-school, family, and women's issues. Her passion is for mothers. She assists her husband in Foundations for Family Success, a ministry for "busy and stretched" families; both do biblical counseling and preventive and instructional workshops. In her rare moments of spare time, she enjoys playing with her children, laughing with her husband, and appreciating God in the ordinary.

Mail:
Foundations for Family Success
c/o Cheryl R. Carter
P.O. Box 712
Long Island, NY 11553-0712
E-mail: Cheryl@momtime.net
Visit her Web sites:
www.momtime.net and www.familysuccess.org